First, We BRUNCH

Recipes and Stories from Victoria's Best-Loved Breakfast Joints

REBECCA WELLMAN

TOUCHWOOD EDITIONS

I'm a simple woman.
I like handsome,
bearded men
and breakfast food.

CONT

Dear Reader,

We didn't do brunch very often when I was a kid, but when I think about it, it conjures up a hazy recollection of a sort of formal affair. There was always a grandma and a grandpa involved, and a wiggle into a fancy dress with patent-leather shoes (which I loved, so that part was okay). It brings up memories of Easter and Mother's Day, and white linen and tulips. My older brother and I always had to behave and be quiet, and I recall a greyish-pink sort of shrimp that tasted vaguely like the stale ice it was laid upon, sort of freezer-burned and tinny. That, and cheesecake in a brown box, for afterwards.

My, how things have changed.

The most astounding thing I discovered as I set out on this mission to write a book about brunch in Victoria was the staggering number of restaurants that offer it. And more keep opening! Existing restaurants keep adding new brunch offerings to their menus, and the people continue to line up. Walk around downtown and its outskirts throughout the day on any weekend (or any weekday, for that matter), and you will undoubtedly run into a lineup of bright-eyed or bedraggled (or a combination of both) customers waiting for their vats of coffee or hair of the dog and a pile of eggs on top of something. With so many brunch options on offer, I think it's safe to say that in this town, brunch is here to stay.

Outside of Victoria, though, perceptions of brunch differ. Consider Sam Sifton from the *New York Times*, for example: "I'd sooner sew buttons than eat or prepare brunch on a Sunday." Or, to my disappointment, my beloved Anthony Bourdain: "Remember, brunch is only served once a week—on the weekends. Buzzword here, 'brunch menu.' Translation? Old, nasty odds and ends, and 12 dollars for two eggs with a free Bloody Mary."

Perhaps that used to be the case. (Remember the grey shrimp?) These days, however, chefs have moved far beyond the week's leftovers. Menus are carefully curated with refined ingredients and dishes that entice both the palate and the eye. By early Friday afternoon, social media is flooded with images of the coming weekend's brunch offerings.

In 2016, Victoria was (unofficially) named the Brunch Capital of Canada by the Food Network's John Catucci. After what I've seen over the course of researching and writing this book, I can verify this sentiment. And it appears that many of you share the same opinion. The order of things seems to be this: First, we brunch; then, and only then, do we go on with whatever else our day brings. It's clear we have priorities.

With a sense of health for our bodies and souls and the importance of sociality, brunch represents gatherings, hangovers, pleasure, sustenance, indulgence, special occasions, conversation, family, new friends and old friends. And all of this can be attained on a lazy Sunday or on a Tuesday afternoon, in just about any part of town.

Having been a food and lifestyle photographer in Victoria for over ten years, I've stood in many kitchens; I know the owners, restaurateurs and chefs in this town well. I've celebrated with them when they found success and commiserated with them when challenges arose. Some of them have become friends, and I can attest to their commitment to quality as well as to the craftsmanship of the food they serve you and the places they serve you in. The recipes in the following pages are gifts from them to us.

First, We Brunch is not only a collection of lovely recipes from a cross-section of Victoria restaurants, but also a great overview of the best places in town to grab breakfast to go. It provides a list of the shops where we can find ingredients to create our own brunch at home and some tips from the experts on all things brunch-related.

I am fully aware that this list is not exhaustive, and I can say with ease that I could have written a second volume and maybe even then not run out of places to write about. I have many favourites out there, as I know you do. This is just a taste—an introduction, perhaps—to the Victoria brunch scene and all it has to offer. I encourage you to flip through this book to find the best places to go out to brunch, to taste and experiment as a home-cook, and to play with these recipes and make them your own.

So, what about those brunch naysayers, anyway? Are they right when they say that brunch is a trendy indulgence? An overrated menu of end-of-the-week leftovers? I'm with John Catucci when he says: "Just shush it. Have an eggs benny and relax."

Where We
SIT
DOWN
TO
EAT

Brunch is a leisure activity. It should be eaten slowly, savoured and enjoyed. A rest between bites, another cup of coffee, the anticipation of a stroll through the neighbourhood afterwards. Gather in twos or tens, catch up over poached eggs, and experience the perfect mid-morning (or afternoon) feast while taking in the scenery. There are plenty of places to choose from in Victoria, and these amazing establishments are but a taste of what Victoria's brunch scene has to offer.

10 ACRES BISTRO

A trio of restaurants in the Inner Harbour reside under the umbrella of the 10 Acres name. The Commons, The Kitchen and The Bistro are all supplied by 10 Acres Farm, an organic and well-rounded farm on the Saanich Peninsula, a mere 25 kilometres away. 10 Acres Bistro is a fun, casual place to hang out for a drink or to meet up with a group for a fantastic meal. With an awesome all-weather patio, a big, wide-open bar, long tables and intimate booths, 10 Acres is bright, bustling and inviting.

Try the Classic Farm Breakfast, with their own house-made bacon and sausage, or the 10 Acres Farm Quiche, with organic farm-grown veggies, asiago and goat cheese.

After brunch, wander down half a block to Government St. for some great shopping, or to the harbour to take a spin on one of the Inner Harbour Ferries—one of the best ways to see the city from a different perspective.

Living on an island means a coastal feast is never far away, and brunch is no exception. With delicious smoky salmon, a creamy hollandaise and a beautiful toasty sourdough, 10 Acres shares with us here a taste of Vancouver Island.

10 ACRES BISTRO

611
COURTNEY STREET
→ 10acres.ca →
250.220.8008

10 Acres Smoked Salmon Eggs Benny

SERVES 4

A lovely change from the typical eggs benny, with sourdough toast and a West Coast twist. You can get some fantastic smoked lox at Finest at Sea (page 252). However, if you order this dish at 10 Acres, you'll get their house-smoked salmon, which is to die for.

TO MAKE THE HOLLANDAISE

Fill the bottom of a double boiler about one-third full with water. Bring the water to a gentle simmer over medium heat. In the top of the double boiler, whisk together the egg yolks, lemon juice, water, Worcestershire sauce and pepper. Set the top over the bottom of the double boiler. Add the melted butter to the egg yolk mixture 1–2 Tbsp at a time, whisking constantly. If the hollandaise begins to get too thick, add a teaspoon or two of hot tap water. Continue whisking until all the butter is incorporated. Whisk in the salt, then remove from the heat. Place a lid on the pan to keep the sauce warm.

TO ASSEMBLE

Poach the eight eggs. (See page 183.) While the eggs are poaching, toast the sourdough and then butter it. Set a piece of sourdough on each of four plates. Top each with smoked salmon and two poached eggs. Pour the hollandaise sauce over the eggs. Sprinkle with red onion and capers and serve immediately.

Hollandaise

4 large egg yolks
3½ Tbsp fresh lemon juice
   (1–2 lemons)
1 Tbsp hot tap water
⅛ tsp Worcestershire sauce
Pinch of ground white pepper
1 cup unsalted butter, melted
¼ tsp kosher salt

To assemble

8 large eggs
4 slices large oval-shaped
   sourdough bread
2 Tbsp unsalted butter, softened
8 oz lox-style wild smoked salmon
½ small red onion, peeled and
   very thinly sliced
4 tsp capers

AGRIUS

I love hanging out in restaurant kitchens—and I'm lucky enough to do it often. As an enthusiastic home chef, I get excited over sous vide machines, giant mixers, fancy knives and specially made refrigerated closets for hocks and shanks and sides. Agrius gives me all of this. Add to that some amazing chefs and bartenders who are all open to chatting about new techniques, the latest seasonal ingredients and the food world in general, and I could easily hang out there all day.

Recently, Agrius was identified as one of the top 100 best restaurants in Canada. Its local focus and organic ingredients list make it so, along with the vast selection of house-made items (a designated charcuterie cooler, rows upon rows of fermented and pickled things, and an endless number of sauces and pâtés and mustards).

Go in and turn right for some of the best cocktails and food in town. Go in and turn left (they share an entrance) to find some of the most amazing pastries, breads and other gorgeous baked delicacies at Agrius's sister and neighbour, Fol Epi (page 222).

Whichever way you turn, you will be surrounded by their beautiful and inviting bright space, excellent food and fantastic and innovative drinks.

AGRIUS

732
YATES STREET
→ agriusrestaurant.com →
778.265.6312

Smoked Ham Hock Terrine Tartine

SERVES 4

> Not everyone is motivated to make their own terrine, but if you are, here is a delicious one. And if you aren't, the good news is that you can buy the rye, the terrine and the sauerkraut at Agrius, take it home and add a fried egg on top. Voilà.

TO MAKE THE SMOKED HAM HOCK TERRINE

Preheat the oven to 300°F if you're planning to use the oven rather than a slow cooker. Line a terrine mould or small loaf pan (about 3 ½ inches × 3 ½ inches × 12 inches) with plastic wrap.

Place the ham hocks, carrots, onion, celery and garlic in a large braising pot or a slow cooker. Just barely cover the vegetables with water and place a tight-fitting lid on top (or cover the pot tightly with aluminum foil).

Place the pot in the oven and cook for 4 hours if using a convection oven; cook for 6–8 hours if using a regular oven (at 300°F) or a slow cooker (on the low setting). The ham hocks are ready when tender and easy to pull away from the bone with a fork or pair of tongs. When cooked, remove 2 cups of the cooking liquid, then set the meat and vegetables aside to cool.

Using two forks, shred the meat, discarding the garlic, pork skin and bones. Place the meat in a large bowl. Dice the cooked carrots, onion and celery and add them to the bowl.

Dissolve the gelatin in the reserved cooking liquid, according to package directions.

Add the parsley, green onions, Dijon and dissolved gelatin to the meat and vegetables.

Transfer the mixture to the prepared terrine mould or loaf pan. Press it firmly into the mould and cover with plastic wrap, making sure the plastic is pressed tightly against the surface of the meat mixture. Refrigerate for 24 hours.

Remove the mould from the refrigerator and slice the terrine to your desired thickness with a sharp knife.

This will keep nicely in an airtight container in the refrigerator for 1–2 weeks.

TO MAKE THE SAUERKRAUT

Using a knife or a mandoline, cut the cabbage quarters into thin strips. Place the cabbage in a very large bowl.

Add the salt to the cabbage, and massage with your hands for 5–10 minutes, or until the cabbage has released a fair amount of liquid. (The amount of liquid released will depend on the cabbage. For example, a fresh cabbage could release

Smoked Ham Hock Terrine

3–4 smoked ham hocks

5 carrots peeled, left whole

1 yellow onion, peeled and quartered

3 ribs of celery, washed and roughly chopped

1 bulb of garlic, peeled and trimmed

5 sheets gelatin, or enough to make 2 cups of liquid (see directions on package)

1 bunch of flat-leaf parsley, washed and chopped (about ¾ cup)

1 bunch of green onions, trimmed and chopped (about ¾ cup)

3 Tbsp grainy Dijon

Sauerkraut

5 lb green cabbage, cored and sliced into quarters

2 Tbsp + 1 ½ tsp kosher salt

To assemble

4 slices rye bread

Grainy mustard

4 eggs, cooked sunny-side up (see page 185)

6 oz fresh greens of your choice

1 Tbsp extra virgin olive oil

1 Tbsp fresh lemon juice (or red wine vinegar)

Salt and ground black pepper

4 small dill pickles

enough liquid to allow the shredded cabbage to be completely submerged. If the cabbage is not quite fresh, you will still get an impressive amount of liquid from it, but you may have to supplement with salt water in order for the shredded cabbage to be completely covered. Dissolve 1 Tbsp salt in 1 cup of hot water. Allow this salt water to cool then add it to the cabbage.)

Stuff the cabbage and its liquid into a fermentation crock or container. Several sterilized 4-cup canning jars can be used if you don't have a crock.

Weigh down the cabbage to submerge the solids in the liquid. Use a plate with a jar of stones on top, or the weight that will often accompany a fermentation vessel. If you are using canning jars, small resealable plastic bags filled with salt water can be placed on top of the cabbage before the lids are put on.

Seal the container with a lid with an airlock (if you don't have one, open the lid every few days to release the carbon dioxide buildup and check for mould).

Store at room temperature (60°F–68°F) for 4–6 weeks. Check every week or so, tasting each time. When ready, the sauerkraut should taste sour and tangy. When the taste is to your satisfaction, transfer to a sterilized jar and top with a non-metallic lid. It will keep nicely in the refrigerator for about 3 months.

TO ASSEMBLE

Remove the ham hock terrine and sauerkraut from the refrigerator and allow to warm up to room temperature (if terrine gets too warm it will start to melt).

Lightly toast the rye bread and spread a layer of mustard over each slice. Place one slice on each of four plates.

Place a generous pile of sauerkraut and a slice of ham hock terrine on each piece of toast. Carefully place a fried egg on top of each terrine.

Dress the greens with the olive oil and lemon juice (or red wine vinegar), and season to taste with salt and pepper. Place some greens and a dill pickle next to the toast on each plate and serve.

Agrius's Carried Away

SERVES
2

Brooke Levie told me about this cocktail, and I can honestly say that I wasn't prepared for how delicious it is. Really? Dijon mustard in a cocktail? Yes, Dijon mustard in a cocktail. It works. Try it. Brooke uses Vancouver Island's Sheringham akvavit when he makes this.

3 oz akvavit
2 oz fino sherry
1 ½ oz celery juice (see sidebar)
   (or ½ a celery stalk, muddled)
1 oz fresh lemon juice
1 oz simple syrup
1 tsp smooth Dijon mustard
Pinch of sea salt
Ice cubes
Celery leaves, for garnish

In a cocktail shaker, combine the akvavit, sherry, celery juice (or muddled ½ stalk of celery), lemon juice, simple syrup, Dijon and salt. Add ice cubes and shake well. Pour into two coupe glasses and garnish with a few celery leaves.

Muddling is the act of extracting the essence or juice from herbs or fruit and vegetables for use in a cocktail. If you can't make celery juice using a juicer, place a roughly chopped ½ celery stalk in a cocktail shaker. Using a wooden muddler or the back of a wooden spoon, press down on the celery until some of the juice has been extracted. You don't want to press too hard—it shouldn't be pulverized, but you do want to see some juice. Add the remainder of the ingredients as outlined above and shake well. Strain through a fine-meshed sieve so you don't get any celery pieces in your drink.

BE LOVE

I am a big fan of Be Love's food, space and philosophy. "High vibration, organic, plant-based cuisine, with natural wines, superfood cocktails and fresh juices made from scratch with love." And the name. Be. Love. Isn't this something we should all strive to be? The pure nourishment of Be Love will surely help.

I first met Joe Cunliffe when he used to come into a tiny restaurant I managed in the Fort Common neighbourhood, before Be Love even existed. I knew that he and his sister, Heather, owned Café Bliss, an awesome café on lower Pandora that served clean vegan fare, with dehydrated crackers and crusts and sauces and magic chocolate treats. It didn't surprise me when I heard that they were opening Be Love as their second spot. They make sure to stud their delicious and healthy food with a beautiful environment, great music, fantastic cocktails and awesome staff. When you go for brunch, be sure to have a Medicinal Chai Tea or a Wellness Toddy, if you want to be set for your virtuous quota for the day.

Everything is free from processed sugar, white flour, gluten, caffeine and dairy products and is easily some of the healthiest (and tastiest) stuff on the planet. Sit outside in the warmer months and be sure to bring in your mason jar to be filled with a smoothie.

BE LOVE

1019
BLANSHARD STREET
— beloverestaurant.ca →
778.433.7181

Be Love's Autumn Benny

A beautiful, fresh version of the traditional benny, this can be made vegan by adding avocado instead of eggs. The cashews require soaking for several hours, so be sure to plan ahead.

TO MAKE THE CASHEW HOLLANDAISE

Soak the cashews in room-temperature water for 4–8 hours, strain and rinse.

Place the soaked cashews, coconut milk, water, lemon juice, olive oil, nutritional yeast, salt, turmeric, white pepper and Italian seasoning in a high-speed blender and blend until smooth.

Transfer the liquid to a small pot and gently warm over low heat before serving, stirring frequently so lumps don't form.

This particular hollandaise will keep in an airtight container in the refrigerator for up to 1 week.

TO MAKE THE ROASTED BUTTERNUT SQUASH ROUNDS

Preheat the oven to 350°F. Line a baking sheet with parchment paper.

Cut the neck of the squash into 1-inch-thick rounds, making at least eight rounds (the neck has no seeds, so there are no holes when you cut it). In a large bowl, toss the squash rounds in the olive oil, maple syrup and salt.

Place the squash rounds on the prepared baking sheet and bake for 30 minutes, or until tender. Remove from the oven and set aside.

TO MAKE THE SAUTÉED MUSHROOMS AND KALE

Add the olive oil to a medium sauté pan over medium-high heat. Add the onion and turn down the heat to medium. Cook until translucent, 5–7 minutes. Add the mushrooms and cook for another 5–7 minutes, until soft. Add the kale and cook for about 2 minutes, just to wilt it. Add salt and pepper to taste.

TO ASSEMBLE

Poach the eggs. (See page 183.) Or you can replace the eggs with avocado slices for a vegan option.

Place two squash rounds on each of the four plates. Divide the sautéed mushroom mixture evenly over the squash rounds. Place one egg (or ¼ avocado for the vegan option) on top of each round and mushroom mixture, Ladle approximately ¼ cup of the warm hollandaise over each egg (or avocado) and serve hot.

Cashew Hollandaise

2 cups raw cashews
¾ cup organic coconut milk (from a can)
¾ cup water
3 Tbsp fresh lemon juice
3 Tbsp extra virgin olive oil
1 Tbsp nutritional yeast
1½ tsp kosher salt
½ tsp ground turmeric
¼ tsp ground white pepper
¼ tsp Italian seasoning

Roasted Butternut Squash Rounds

1–2 butternut squash with large necks
2 Tbsp extra virgin olive oil
2 Tbsp maple syrup (any grade except pancake syrup)
¼ tsp kosher salt

Sautéed Mushrooms and Kale

1–2 Tbsp olive oil
½ medium red onion, sliced
½ lb mushrooms (chanterelle, oyster or cremini), sliced
1 bunch of kale, tough stems removed, and sliced
Salt and ground black pepper

To assemble

8 large eggs or 2 avocados, sliced

Be Love's Naramata Spritz

SERVES
2

A light and sparkling cocktail, this is lovely on a summer patio. The elderflower adds a floral note that goes perfectly with a Sauvignon.

6 oz dry, acidic white wine, such as Sauvignon-Semillon
1 oz St-Germain elderflower liqueur
Ice cubes
Soda water
2 orange twists, for garnish

Divide the white wine and St-Germain evenly between two red wine glasses. Stir. Fill with ice, top with soda water and garnish with a long orange twist.

Be Love, along with many other popular restaurants, coffee shops and retail shops, sits within the Fort Common District, an area that spans the block at the corner of Blanshard and Fort Sts. The Fort Common itself is a revitalized brick carriage courtyard, made into an urban outdoor venue for retreats, weddings and summertime events. When the sun comes out, The Fort Common, accessed via a lit brick alleyway between Be Love and Starbucks on Blanshard St., becomes an inviting outdoor seating area for the surrounding restaurants and shops.

BLUE CRAB
SEAFOOD HOUSE

Having been a morning server at the Blue Crab, I can say without a doubt that I gained a good deal of my breakfast experience there. Serving breakfast is unlike serving any other meal. People are hungry. They need coffee. It goes quickly, as folks typically want to get on with their day. I loved it, though, and the Blue Crab was a picturesque place to spend my mornings, to say the least. The restaurant lives in the Coast Victoria Hotel and Marina, which sits on Victoria's outer harbour, providing a great view to diners of float planes taking off, ferries heading to the US, gigantic private yachts floating by, Victoria's harbour ferries, affectionately known as "pickle boats," and the odd sea otter or seal frolicking in the rocks.

This is where I warmed my hands on the pass, warding off the morning chill, as the breakfast cooks scrambled eggs by the dozen, building bennies and hashes and topping all sorts of good things with Dungeness crab and smoked salmon. High stacks of pancakes and French toast with fruit compote. Sweet and savoury, the smell of coffee, the '70s playlist on the stereo and the sounds of the espresso machine steaming away. It was a good place to be.

I consider the Blue Crab to have some of the best seafood in town, and whether it's dinner, lunch or breakfast, you will always find a taste of it there.

BLUE CRAB SEAFOOD HOUSE
in the Coast Victoria Hotel and Marina by APA

146
KINGSTON STREET
bluecrab.ca →
250.480.1999

Blue Crab Benny

> I love these crab cakes, so I consider it a big win that Chef Gabe is letting me share this recipe with you.

TO MAKE THE CRAB CAKES

Place the panko, flour and egg in three separate shallow bowls. Set aside. Line a cookie sheet with parchment paper.

Bring a large pot of water to a boil over high heat. Stir in the shrimp, salt, parsley, bay leaf and lemon zest. Bring back to a boil, then remove from the heat and place a lid on the pot. Depending on the size of the shrimp, let sit in the covered pot for 5 minutes. Break open one shrimp to ensure it is opaque and cooked through. If it isn't, return it to the pot for another 1–2 minutes. When the shrimp are ready, drain and rinse them under cold water, and discard all the other ingredients from the pot.

Peel the shrimp and place them in a food processor fitted with the steel blade. Pulse until the meat is pulverized but not pasty. You want a bit of texture. Scrape the shrimp meat out of the food processor and into a large bowl. Add the crab, bell pepper, fresh breadcrumbs, chopped herbs, mayonnaise and cayenne. Taste and adjust for seasoning. Gently fold all the ingredients together. Using your hands, form eight evenly sized crab cakes, 1 ½–2 inches across. Dip each cake in the flour, then whisked egg, then panko to completely coat. Set aside on a large plate.

Preheat the oven to 350°F.

Add the butter and olive oil to a large cast iron or non-stick pan over medium-high heat. Cook the crab cakes in batches, allowing each one to get lightly browned on one side, before flipping, 3–5 minutes per side. Add additional butter or olive oil to the pan as needed. Place the cooked crab cakes on the prepared cookie sheet and place in the oven to warm through before serving.

TO MAKE THE HOLLANDAISE

Place the wine in a small pot over high heat and add the tarragon, thyme, peppercorns, salt and shallot. Bring to a boil, then turn down the heat to a simmer and cook for 20–30 minutes, until the wine has reduced to about ¼ cup. Remove from the heat, strain and discard the solids. Set the wine aside.

Set a large pot with 2–3 inches of water in it over high heat, and bring the water to a simmer. Place the egg yolks in a metal bowl along with the wine reduction and whisk together. Place the metal bowl on top of the simmering pot, ensuring

Crab Cakes

1 cup panko breadcrumbs
⅓ cup all-purpose flour
1 egg, whisked
¼ lb fresh, raw shrimp, tails and shells left on
1 tsp kosher salt
1 large sprig fresh flat-leaf parsley
1 bay leaf
1 large intact peel of lemon zest (the equivalent of about 1 Tbsp)
½ lb picked and cleaned Dungeness crab (if you are using frozen crab, be sure to squeeze all the moisture out of it)
½ medium red bell pepper, finely diced
½ cup finely chopped fresh breadcrumbs
¼ cup mixed fresh herbs, finely chopped (thyme, any type of parsley, chives and tarragon are all good)
¼ cup good-quality full-fat mayonnaise
¼ tsp cayenne pepper
Salt
2 Tbsp unsalted butter
1 Tbsp olive oil

Hollandaise

1 cup dry white wine
1 sprig fresh tarragon
1 sprig fresh thyme
2 white peppercorns
Pinch of kosher salt
1 tsp diced shallot

the bottom of the bowl does not touch the water in the pot.

Whisk the yolks and reduction together for about 1 minute, until the mixture doubles in size. Very slowly, in a thin drizzle, add the clarified butter, continuing to whisk until a mayonnaise-like consistency is achieved. (You may not need all the butter.) Remove from the heat and then gently fold in the lemon juice, Tabasco, Worcestershire, salt and white pepper to taste. Cover with a lid and set aside.

TO ASSEMBLE

Poach the eggs. (See page 183.)

Split and toast the English muffins. Butter each side, and place two muffin halves on each of four warm plates. Divide the spinach (raw, as in the photo, or sautéed) evenly between the muffin halves. Top the spinach with a crab cake, poached egg and hollandaise, and garnish with dill or parsley.

4 egg yolks
¾ cup clarified butter, kept warm (see page 189)
1 Tbsp fresh lemon juice
Dash of Tabasco sauce
Dash of Worcestershire sauce
Salt
Pinch of ground white pepper

To assemble
8 large eggs
4 English muffins
Butter for the muffins
A handful of fresh spinach
Fresh dill or chopped curly parsley, for garnish

CAFÉ VENETO

The bar at Veneto is in the Rialto Hotel, right in Victoria's downtown core, and it is one of my favourite places to go for cocktails. Many a night has been spent there with friends, sipping a Rosemary's Baby or a Corpse Reviver 2, or sometimes a flight of old Hemingway creations. We go there pre-dinner, pre-show or often times at the end of the night, to cap it off. It holds many memories of birthdays celebrated, running into old friends and just hanging out, learning from the experts behind the bar.

The little Café Veneto is right next door and offers all the remedies that the aftermath of the night before calls for. There is something extra fun about returning to the scene of the crime, this time to indulge in giant coffees, savoury waffles and all sorts of eggs. If you're from out of town, Café Veneto is in the perfect spot to spend the morning before heading out for a walking tour. Head down Pandora to the Wharf St. waterfront, or explore the shops along Government St. Or if a slow morning is more what you have in mind, grab a window seat at Café Veneto and order yourself another latte.

CAFÉ VENETO

653

PANDORA AVENUE

cafeveneto.ca →

250.383.4157

Veggie Benny on Cheddar and Chive Waffles

SERVES 4 - 6

Several components go into this decadent dish, but the jam and red pepper sauce can be made ahead, which makes it easier. Both of these are great to have stowed away in the refrigerator for sure, so double the recipe if you are so inclined.

TO MAKE THE TOMATO AND CARAMELIZED ONION JAM

In a heavy-bottomed pot, melt the butter over medium-high heat. Add the onions and sauté for 20–30 minutes, until browned and caramelized. Add the water and scrape any brown bits off the bottom of the pan. Continue cooking, stirring occasionally, for about 15 minutes, until most of the water has evaporated. Add the tomatoes, brown sugar, white sugar, lemon juice, apple cider vinegar, salt and red pepper flakes. Stir to combine. Bring to a boil, then turn down the heat to simmer, stirring occasionally, for about 20 minutes, until the tomatoes have broken down and the mixture has a jam-like consistency. Scrape into a bowl and set aside. Tomato jam can be kept in an airtight container in the refrigerator for up to 3 days. Gently warm over low heat before serving.

TO MAKE THE SMOKED RED PEPPER SAUCE

In a blender or food processor fitted with the steel blade, place the roasted red peppers, onion, vinegar, garlic, honey, mustard and chipotle purée. Pulse until broken up and starting to become smooth. With the machine running, add the oil in a slow trickle and allow to emulsify, pulsing and scraping down the sides when necessary. Continue to blend until very smooth. Push the mixture through a fine mesh sieve into a bowl to strain out any leftover chunky bits. Season to taste with salt and pepper and set aside. This can be kept in an airtight container in the refrigerator for up to 3 days or in the freezer for up to 3 months.

TO MAKE THE CHEDDAR AND CHIVE WAFFLES

Preheat the oven to 250°F.

In a large bowl, mix the flour, baking powder, baking soda and salt with the cheddar and chives. In a small, deep bowl, beat the egg whites with a handheld mixer until soft peaks form. In a medium bowl, whisk the egg yolks with the milk and butter until well combined.

Add the milk mixture to the dry ingredients and mix with a wooden spoon until just combined. Using a wide spatula, fold in the egg whites until just blended.

Tomato and Caramelized Onion Jam

MAKES 2 CUPS

2 Tbsp unsalted butter
2 large yellow onions, thinly sliced
½ cup water
3 lb Roma tomatoes cored, seeded and finely chopped (skin on)
½ cup brown sugar, packed
½ cup granulated sugar
¼ cup fresh lemon juice
¼ cup apple cider vinegar
2 tsp kosher salt
1 tsp red pepper flakes

Smoked Red Pepper Sauce

MAKES 1 CUP

2 cups roasted red bell peppers (store-bought is okay)
¼ cup roughly chopped red onion
2 Tbsp red wine vinegar
1 Tbsp crushed garlic
1 Tbsp honey
2 tsp Dijon mustard
2 tsp chipotle adobo purée
⅓ cup vegetable oil
Salt and ground black pepper

Cheddar and Chive Waffles

MAKES 6–8 WAFFLES

2 cups all-purpose flour
2 tsp baking powder
½ tsp baking soda
¼ tsp kosher salt
1 cup grated medium cheddar
⅓ cup minced chives
2 large eggs, separated

Heat a waffle iron and brush it with oil or butter.

Spoon 1 cup of batter onto the iron and cook according to the machine directions. Keep the waffles warm in the oven until ready to serve.

TO ASSEMBLE

While the waffles are keeping warm in the oven, poach two eggs per guest. (See page 183.) Place one warm waffle on each plate. Top with tomato onion jam, spinach, avocado, two poached eggs and hollandaise sauce. Drizzle with smoked red pepper sauce, top with chives and serve hot.

2 cups whole milk
¼ cup salted butter, melted
   and cooled

To assemble
2 cups baby spinach
2 avocados, sliced
8–12 eggs, depending on how many
   guests you have
2 cups warm hollandaise sauce
   (see page 189)
2 Tbsp finely chopped chives

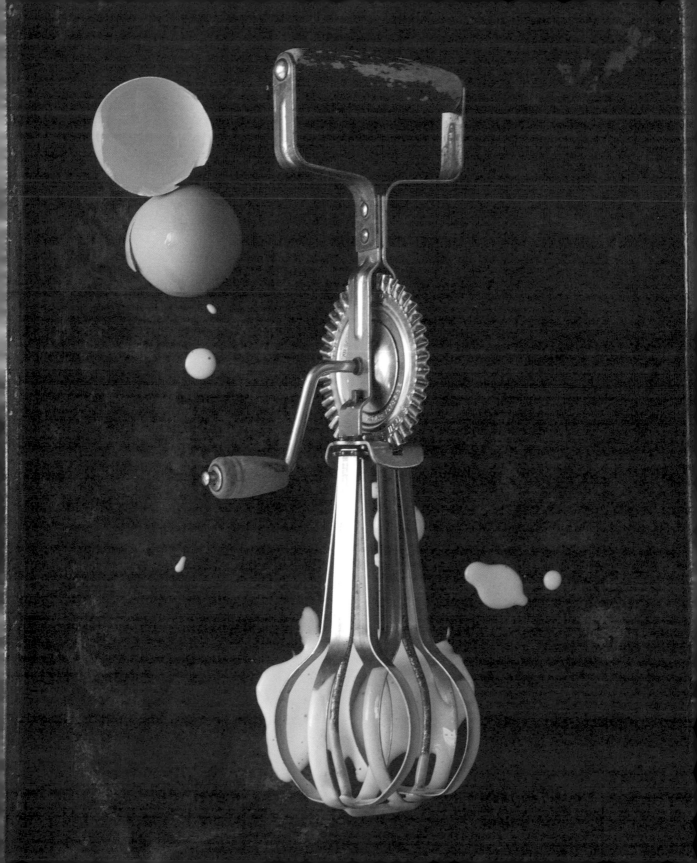

CANOE BREWPUB

Canoe Brewpub is one of the most beautiful places in town— not only for taking photos in, but also to stop by for a drink or a meal. Housed in a huge heritage brick building on the downtown waterfront with rustic wooden floors, crystal chandeliers, timber frames, a big, gorgeous seaside deck, live music and their own brewery onsite pumping out some great hand-crafted small-batch beer, the place is impressive in so many ways. Canoe is bright and warm, timeless and current, expansive and intimate. I don't know what's better: spending some time on its giant patio in the sunshine with a brew, soaking up Victoria's oceanside scenery, or sitting inside the pub, taking in the latest live band, enjoying some delicious food and catching up with good friends. And now that brunch has been added to the menu, we've all got another excuse to head down to Canoe to grab a bite, take in the scene and revel in all it has to offer.

CANOE BREWPUB

450 SWIFT STREET
→ canoebrewpub.com →
250.361.1940

Prosciutto and Asparagus Brunch Salad

SERVES 4

A very fresh salad that clearly announces the arrival of spring, this bright and colourful dish is made brunchy with a soft poached egg and a gorgeous choron sauce on top. Choron is a twist on a béarnaise sauce, made with tomatoes and a splash of lemon.

TO MAKE THE CHORON SAUCE

In a small pot over medium-high heat, combine the water, vinegar, pinch of salt and pinch of paprika. Bring to a simmer for 7–10 minutes, until reduced by half. Let cool.

In a stainless steel bowl, whisk together the vinegar reduction and egg yolks. Set the bowl over a pot of simmering water over low heat, ensuring the bottom of the bowl does not touch the water. Whisk constantly, until ribbons form in the mixture. This will happen very quickly. Remove from the heat and very, very slowly trickle in the clarified butter, continuing to whisk until the mixture becomes thick and creamy. Whisk in the sundried tomatoes, lemon juice and Tabasco. Season to taste with salt and pepper. Cover with a lid to keep warm.

TO MAKE THE SALAD

Bring a shallow pan of water to a boil over high heat. Add the asparagus, and cook for 1–2 minutes, until just tender. Remove from the heat, drain the water, season to taste with salt and pepper and return to the pan. Cover to keep warm.

Poach the eggs. (See page 183.)

Toss the arugula with the lemon juice and olive oil. Season to taste with salt and pepper and divide between four plates. Top each plate with asparagus, prosciutto, goat cheese, hazelnuts and tomatoes. Place one egg on top of each salad. Ladle choron sauce overtop and serve.

Choron Sauce

6 Tbsp water

2 Tbsp white vinegar

Pinch of kosher salt

Pinch of paprika

6 egg yolks

3 cups clarified butter (see page 189)

4 Tbsp sundried tomatoes, very finely chopped (see sidebar)

1 tsp fresh lemon juice

Tabasco sauce to taste

Salt and ground black pepper

Salad

16 spears asparagus, trimmed and washed

4 large eggs

4 loosely packed cups arugula

1 Tbsp fresh lemon juice

1 tsp extra virgin olive oil

Salt and ground black pepper

12 slices prosciutto, roughly torn into bite-sized pieces

6 oz goat cheese, crumbled

½ cup toasted hazelnuts, roughly chopped

12 cherry tomatoes, cut in half

If you're using dried sundried tomatoes, reconstitute them in boiling water for 15 minutes before chopping. If you're using sundried tomatoes in oil, drain them well before chopping.

CHARLOTTE & THE QUAIL

A sweet and whimsical little restaurant, Charlotte & the Quail is tucked in the midst of a magical garden. You may not know that Charlotte & the Quail is Nourish's (page 114) big sister. Or rather, her grandmother, as made evident by the patterned cushions, unmatched vintage plateware and afternoon tea sort of vibe. The food, however, is not even close to that of teahouses of yore, with its hipster-healthy feel, out-of-this-world, ever-changing menu, and firm focus on local and seasonal ingredients. They even have a retail area where they sell beautiful aprons, fabric bags and their famous Sleeping Beauty Pancake mix, among other delicacies. Their peaceful garden porch is the perfect retreat from the hustle and bustle of the day, complete with a visit from Charlotte the cat, the restaurant's friendly namesake, and a view of the funny little quails running through the flowers and trees.

CHARLOTTE & THE QUAIL

505
QUAYLE ROAD
— charlotteandthequail.ca →
250.590.6346

Green Pie

SERVES 8-10

This pie, part quiche and part frittata, is fantastic. It's super versatile in that you can use up all your greens from the garden or the refrigerator and the flour creates the impression of a crust without having to make anything separately. The gluten-free flour blend can be purchased right at Charlotte's, but you can use your preferred brand, or even regular all-purpose flour, if you like.

10 cups fresh greens (chard, kale or spinach, or a combination)
1 small yam, skin on, sliced into rounds about ¼ inch thick
3 Tbsp olive oil, divided
Salt and ground black pepper
1 Tbsp unsalted butter
1 large yellow onion, thinly sliced
6 eggs
2 cups whole milk
1½ tsp sea salt
1½ cups Charlotte & the Quail gluten-free flour blend
3 tsp baking powder
¼ cup diced green onions
¼ cup chopped soft herbs (dill, any type of parsley, thyme, garlic and chives all work well)

Preheat the oven to 400°F. Line a cookie sheet with parchment paper.

Place a large pot on the stove over medium-high heat and add 2 Tbsp of water. Add all of the fresh greens to the pot. Bring the water to a boil and, using tongs, toss the greens around the pot for about 8 minutes, until wilted. Remove from the heat and place the greens in a colander in the sink. Let cool. Using your hands, squeeze any excess moisture from the greens. Chop roughly and set aside.

Toss the yam slices in 1 Tbsp of the olive oil, being sure to coat all sides. Season to taste with salt and pepper and place in a single layer on the prepared cookie sheet—no overlapping! Roast in the oven for 15–20 minutes, or until almost cooked through.

Meanwhile, heat another 1 Tbsp olive oil and the butter in a large frying pan over medium-high heat. Add the onions and stir to coat. Season to taste with salt and pepper. Continue to cook, stirring frequently, for 20–30 minutes, until the onions are softened and caramelized. Remove from the heat and set aside.

Remove the yams from the oven and set aside.

In a large bowl, place the eggs, milk and remaining 1 Tbsp olive oil. Add the salt, flour and baking powder and whisk together until blended.

Cover the bottom of a deep-dish 9-inch pie plate with the cooked greens, green onions and chopped fresh herbs. Layer the caramelized onions overtop and then pour the egg mixture over them. Place the yam slices on top of the whole surface.

Bake for 30–40 minutes, or until the centre of the pie is firm. Remove from the oven and let sit for about 10 minutes before serving.

Charlotte & the Quail sits on the edge of Glendale Gardens and Woodlands, at the Horticulture Centre of the Pacific. The centre comprises 103 acres of gorgeous and varying local garden species, so you will be sure to come across some unique plants here. Before or after brunch, take a wander through the garden paths. Charlotte's Dandelion Latte and Water Kefir are perfect garden strolling accompaniments.

DEMITASSE

Demitasse is the perfect place to either sit and stay or grab and go. Not only is it nestled in a sweet residential area of Oak Bay, but it also houses one of the best little garden centres around. Here, you can grab a coffee and some breakfast and sit right in the garden, surrounded by the unique flowers, trees and plants that Demitasse has become known for, as well as by some old favourites. Bay trees hover above, anemones and hellebores nod their pretty heads in your direction, and boxwoods and maidenhair ferns grab at your ankles as you wander through. I was introduced to Demitasse years ago, and I was taken aback by its vast array of delicious food items. Quiches, pies, sweets, salads, sandwiches and even pizza adorn their shelves and fridges. Nothing is the same from day to day, as a team of talented chefs creates mouth-watering dishes every morning from scratch. You'll find fresh local farm garlic, little flower bouquets from Cultivated by Christin (a local urban organic flower farmer right in Oak Bay) and other seasonal delights straight from the fields.

DEMITASSE

2164
MCNEILL AVENUE

demitasse.ca →

250.598.6668

Spanish Frittata

SERVES 4-6

> "Frittata" comes from the Italian *fritto*, which means "fried." It is a great way to use up those leftovers from last night's BBQ party—potatoes, grilled vegetables and anything else that needs a new home can be tossed in. This is the perfect accompaniment to the farro salad (below).

1 Tbsp unsalted butter
2 cups boiled potatoes, cut into ¾-inch dice (skin on or off)
2 oz mixed pitted olives, chopped
2 oz sundried tomatoes in oil, chopped
2 oz sprouting purple broccoli, blanched and cut into large pieces (or regular broccoli or another favourite green)
8 large eggs, whisked
½ cup shaved Manchego cheese, divided

Preheat the broiler to low.

Heat a 12-inch cast iron pan, or a non-stick oven-safe pan, over medium-high heat. Melt the butter in the pan, add the diced potatoes and fry for about 10 minutes, until golden brown. Add the olives, sundried tomatoes and broccoli (or other green) and cook, stirring, for 2–3 minutes, until the green vegetables are softened. Pour the eggs over the whole mixture, and then add half the Manchego cheese. Cook, stirring, for 3–4 minutes, or until the eggs just begin to set. Place the pan under the broiler for 3–4 minutes, until the frittata is slightly browned and completely set. Remove from the broiler and scatter the rest of the Manchego cheese overtop before serving.

SERVES 4-6

Warm Farro, Asparagus and Portobello Mushroom Salad

> This recipe goes well with the frittata (above) and also stands well on its own. If you don't have asparagus and portobellos on hand, not to worry..Any leftover grilled veg works perfectly.

½ cup farro
1 tsp extra virgin olive oil
Salt and ground black pepper
10 stalks of asparagus (thin stalks are nice for this recipe), grilled and chopped
2 portobello mushrooms, stems and gills removed, grilled and sliced
Juice and zest of ½ lemon
⅓ cup shaved Manchego cheese

Place the farro and 1 ¼ cups water in a medium pot over high heat. Bring to a boil, then turn down the heat to a simmer, cover and cook for 20–25 minutes, or until the water is fully absorbed. Turn off the heat and allow the farro to rest, still covered, for 10 minutes. Remove the lid, add the olive oil, season to taste with salt and pepper and fluff with a fork. Place the farro in a serving bowl and add the asparagus, portobello mushrooms, lemon juice and lemon zest. Season to taste with salt and pepper and garnish with the Manchego cheese.

FANTASTICO BAR-DELI

Over the years that I've lived in Victoria, I have become acquainted with Fantastico in a number of ways. One, as a lover of their coffee. Whether I'm in need of a cup on the run or somewhere to meet up with friends, Fantastico is usually where I find myself. Two, as a fan of their three locations, each with unique and tasteful combinations of food, beer, wine, atmosphere and accessibility. And three, as a commercial client of theirs, when I helped run a teeny restaurant downtown. We served Fantastico coffee, and their impeccable service standard combined with the quality of their product is something I will never forget.

Just on the edge of downtown, in Quadra Village, is Caffe Fantastico. The mother ship of the three, this location is where the roastery lives and where Fantastico really began to flourish. (Prior to this, from 1993, Fantastico could be found at a coffee cart on Victoria's Inner Harbour.) The lingering scent of roasting coffee wafts throughout the café, mingling with the aroma of freshly baked sweets and savouries. You can grab a latte with breakfast or a local brew with an early dinner. On the opposite edge of town in the Parkside Hotel is Tre Fantastico, which serves excellent daytime fare and is also open late, making it a great place to grab a fantastic meal with a glass of local wine.

The location I'll focus on here, though, is Fantastico bar-deli, in Vic West, in an eco-friendly, community-focused development in a formerly industrial area of town. Allow me to paint the scene: After a leisurely bike ride on "The Goose" (the local name for the Galloping Goose Trail), you stop in and choose from an impressive selection of cheeses and cured meats. You sit down for a latte or a cider and a chat with Natalie, the resident cheese

and local preserves. You take a peek into the grab-and-go refrigerator for fresh eggs and house-made tapenade, hummus and pickles. You're hungry, so you order a Breakfast Melt with Whole Beast bacon. Back on your bike, your pannier (and belly) full, you're on your way, smiling and satisfied.

expert, about the new wheel that has just arrived from the Netherlands. You peruse diverse items on the grocery shelf, such as house-made granola

CAFFE FANTASTICO
965
KINGS ROAD
250.385.2326

FANTASTICO BAR-DELI
102-398
HARBOUR ROAD
250.590.2315

TRE FANTASTICO
810
HUMBOLDT STREET
— caffefantastico.com →
250.590.8014

FANTASTICO BAR-DELI

Fantastico bar-deli's Breakfast Melt

SERVES AS MANY GUESTS AS YOU COOK FOR

This isn't a recipe so much as a gathering of the best local ingredients and products, all fresh and made with love. Aristotle was right when he said, "The whole is greater than the sum of its parts." For this recipe try a lovely goat milk Honey Bee gouda, available for purchase at Fantastico bar-deli, bread from Fol Epi (page 222) and bacon from The Whole Beast (page 278). Check out the other Fantasticos as well for a variety of delicious breakfast dishes.

Goat milk gouda
Sliced whole wheat bread
Large eggs
Bacon
Fresh sliced tomatoes
Fresh sliced avocado
Sea salt and ground black pepper

Lay slices of cheese on slices of bread, place them on a cookie sheet and pop them into a hot oven, until the bread is toasted and the cheese is melted. Fry some eggs (see page 185). Fry or bake some bacon. Top the cheese toast with tomatoes, avocado, bacon and egg, in whatever order and numbers you like. Season with salt and pepper, grab a latte and enjoy!

FLOYD'S DINER

FLOYD'S DINER

866
YATES STREET
250.381.5114

721
STATION AVE., LANGFORD BC
778.440.1200

——— floydsdiner.ca —→

Floyd's is an upbeat, colourful, fun place, with delicious food and lots of smiling faces. Give yourself lots of time here, as simply reading their menu, full of tributes to regular customers, celebrity quotes and a whole lot of musings, is entertainment in itself. This bright breakfast joint is a classic Victoria institution—you can't miss its red-orange building on the corner of Quadra and Yates. You'll find not only food classics such as bennies and chicken waffles here, but also photographs of icons such as Monroe and Chaplin and Presley adorning the walls, giving the space an "Old Pop's Shoppe" sort of feel. Old tunes blast through the speakers, bringing back memories of teenage joy and angst simultaneously (Abba, Journey, Chicago) and recollections of hanging out all day, drinking coffee and eating pancakes. Meet friends, chat about your weekend and before you know it, breakfast has morphed into lunch and you need the menu again. Floyd's is a happy place. You walk in and immediately feel at home. And it really wouldn't surprise me at all to learn that when Elvis left the building, this is where he went.

Herb Hudson Chicken Waffles

SERVES 4-6

Roscoe's House of Chicken and Waffles is a famous soul food restaurant that was opened in Los Angeles in 1975 by a fellow named Herb Hudson. Celebrities like Natalie Cole and Redd Foxx frequented Roscoe's and spread the word about the unusual food combination to their celebrity friends, soon making it a well-known institution. If you pay attention, you will hear its name pop up in many movies and TV shows, such as Quentin Tarantino's *Jackie Brown* and the '90s sitcom *The Fresh Prince of Bel-Air*. It is one of rapper Snoop Dogg's favourite restaurants. This recipe is Floyd's tribute to Herb himself.

TO MAKE THE RED CURRANT JALAPEÑO JELLY

Preheat the oven to 375°F.

Place the jalapeños on a small baking tray and roast for about 40 minutes, until brown. Remove from the oven and let cool. Chop roughly and place in a food processor fitted with the steel blade. Add the red currant jelly and lemon juice, and blend until smooth. Set aside. This will keep in an airtight container in the refrigerator for up to 3 days.

TO MAKE THE HOLLANDAISE

Vigorously whisk the egg yolks, lemon juice and white wine together in a stainless steel bowl until the mixture is thickened and doubled in volume. Place the bowl over a pot of barely simmering water (or use a double boiler) over low heat. The water should not touch the bottom of the bowl. Whisk rapidly, being careful not to let the eggs get too hot or they will scramble. Immediately, and very slowly, drizzle in the melted butter and continue to whisk until the sauce is thickened and doubled in volume again. Remove from the heat and whisk in the salt. Cover to keep warm until ready to use.

TO MAKE THE CHICKEN

Preheat the oven to 200°F. Line a plate with paper towel. Line a cookie sheet with parchment paper.

Cut the chicken breasts evenly into 1- to 2-inch strips and pat dry. In a bowl, combine the flour, onion powder, garlic powder, cayenne pepper, paprika and salt and blend well.

In a large, deep pot over high heat, bring at least 3 inches of vegetable oil to 350°F (use a kitchen thermometer to check the temperature). Place the beaten egg in a small bowl. Dredge each piece of chicken through the egg, then through

Red Currant Jalapeño Jelly
3 jalapeños
½ cup red currant jelly
2 Tbsp fresh lemon juice

Hollandaise
4 egg yolks
1 Tbsp fresh lemon juice
1 Tbsp dry white wine
½ cup clarified butter (page 189)
Pinch of sea salt

Chicken
2 (each 6 oz) boneless, skinless chicken breasts
¼ cup all-purpose flour
1 Tbsp onion powder
1 Tbsp garlic powder
1 tsp cayenne pepper
1 tsp paprika
1 tsp sea salt
1 egg, beaten
Vegetable oil, for frying

Waffles
1½ cups all-purpose flour
1½ tsp baking powder
Pinch of sea salt
2 Tbsp granulated sugar
1½ cups 2% milk
2 large eggs
3 Tbsp unsalted butter, melted, plus extra for waffle iron

the flour mixture. In batches of four or five, gently drop the chicken strips into the hot oil and cook completely, 3–4 minutes, flipping about halfway through. Set the chicken on the prepared plate to drain off any excess oil. Transfer to the prepared cookie sheet and keep warm in the oven until ready to serve.

TO MAKE THE WAFFLES

Preheat a waffle iron.

In a large bowl, combine the flour, baking powder, salt and sugar. In another bowl, beat together the milk and eggs. Whisk this into the dry ingredients until just combined. Stir in the 3 Tbsp melted butter. Brush the hot waffle iron with more melted butter. Spoon about ½ cup of batter onto the iron and close to cook until golden brown. Remove to a plate and keep warm in the oven with the chicken.

TO ASSEMBLE

Heat a frying pan over medium-high heat. Line a plate with paper towel.

Cook the bacon until crispy, place it on the prepared plate to absorb any excess oil and then chop roughly.

Poach the eggs. (See page 183.)

Place a waffle on each of four to six warm plates. Roughly chop the cooked chicken and divide it evenly over the waffles. Place some chopped bacon on top of the chicken. Place two eggs on each plate. Cover the eggs with hollandaise and drizzle red currant jelly over the entire dish. Garnish with scallions and serve immediately.

To assemble
4–6 strips of bacon
8–12 large eggs
Chopped scallions, for garnish

FUEGO OLD TOWN EATERY

If you are familiar with Café Mexico, in all of its latest post-fire glory, then you may also know Fuego Old Town Eatery, Café Mexico's little sister and next-door neighbour. After a devastating fire in early 2015 that took Café Mexico down to its bare bones, owners Brad and Hilda Olberg, who have run Café Mexico since 1985, recognized that they had some rather daunting long-term work ahead of them, and opened Fuego as a fill-in to keep a corner of the space active and alive. It has since become a sweet little destination in its own right, offering breakfasts and lunches that reflect the Café Mexico charm and flavours. You'll recognize the décor, inspired by Café Mexico, in this rustic yet homey space, and besides their full array of Latin inspired dishes, you'll get to enjoy their homemade hot sauce. (Spoiler: it's awesome.)

After brunch at Fuego, visit Market Square right outside the back door. It's an open, colourful (in look and feel) square with many charming shops to peruse. Seasonally, you'll find live music, buskers and all sorts of entertainment.

FUEGO
OLD TOWN EATERY

1435
STORE STREET

fuegooldtowneatery.com

250.590.2177

Eggs Mollete

Pronounced "mo letty," this is a perfect breakfast for any day of the week. Cook the eggs whichever way you like best.

TO MAKE THE JALAPEÑO CORNBREAD

Preheat the oven to 350°F. Grease a 9-inch square baking pan.

In a large mixing bowl, whisk together the flour, cornmeal, sugar, baking powder and salt. In a separate bowl, whisk together the eggs, buttermilk and butter. Add the corn, cheese and jalapeños and mix well to combine. Pour this wet mixture into the dry mixture, and mix until just blended. Do not overmix.

Spoon the thick batter into the prepared pan and bake for 40–45 minutes, until brown on top and fairly firm to the touch. Remove from the oven and let cool in the pan.

TO MAKE THE REFRIED BEANS

In a medium pot, heat the vegetable oil over medium-low heat and sauté the onions, garlic and chili flakes for about 5 minutes, until the onions are translucent but not browned.

Add the pinto beans, chicken stock and chicken base and bring to a boil. Turn down the heat and allow the mixture to simmer for 5 minutes, stirring occasionally. Remove from the heat and add salt to taste. Let cool slightly and mash with a handheld mixer or fork until some beans are smooth and others remain chunky. The final texture is up to you! Set aside.

TO MAKE THE PICO DE GALLO

In a medium bowl, mix together the tomatoes, onion, jalapeños, cilantro, lime juice and salt. Add pepper to taste.

TO MAKE THE GUACAMOLE

Cut the avocados in half and scoop the flesh into a large bowl. Add the onions, cilantro, jalapeños, and ½ cup of jalapeño juice or hot sauce and lime juice to taste. Mix well and season to taste with salt and pepper.

TO ASSEMBLE

Preheat the oven to 350°F. Line a baking sheet with parchment paper.

Cut the cornbread into four pieces, remove from the pan and then slice each piece through the middle like a hamburger bun to give you eight pieces of cornbread.

Jalapeño Cornbread
Butter for greasing pan
2½ cups all-purpose flour
1½ cups cornmeal
¼ cup granulated sugar
3 Tbsp baking powder
½ tsp kosher salt
3 large eggs, lightly beaten
2 cups buttermilk
¼ cup unsalted butter,
   melted and cooled
1 cup fresh or frozen corn niblets
1 cup grated Monterey Jack cheese
½ cup de-seeded and minced
   jalapeños

Refried Beans
¼ cup vegetable oil
½ cup finely diced yellow onion
1 large garlic clove, minced
1 Tbsp chili flakes
3 (each 19 oz) cans pinto beans,
   drained and rinsed
2½ cups chicken or vegetable stock
1 Tbsp chicken or vegetable
   bouillon base
Salt

Pico de Gallo
2 Roma tomatoes, finely diced
1 small white onion, finely diced
2–3 jalapeños, seeded and finely
   diced
1 Tbsp chopped cilantro
1 Tbsp fresh lime juice
½ tsp kosher salt
Ground black pepper

Place the pieces, cut side up, on the prepared baking sheet and spread 1 tsp butter on each piece. Toast in the oven for about 15 minutes.

While the bread is toasting, poach, fry or scramble the eggs. (See page 185 or page 186.) Place two pieces of cornbread on each of four plates. Pour ¼– ½ cup warm refried beans on each slice. If you have leftover beans, cool completely and store them in an airtight container in the refrigerator for up to 3 days or freeze for up to 3 months. Divide the Monterey Jack cheese evenly overtop the warm beans right away so that it begins to melt. (Place the plates in the oven for about 2 minutes if you need to melt the cheese further.)

Top each plate with two eggs, pico de gallo and guacamole. Garnish with cilantro and serve with the hot sauce of your choosing.

Guacamole

4 ripe avocados
½ cup finely diced onions
½ cup chopped cilantro
½ cup seeded and minced jalapeños
3 Tbsp fresh lime juice
Salt and ground black pepper

To assemble

Butter
8 large eggs
1 ½ cups shredded Monterey
   Jack cheese
Cilantro sprigs, for garnish
Your favourite hot sauce

Fuego's Michelada

SERVES
6

> Maggi Seasoning Sauce adds a special touch of umami to this drink. Look for the yellow- and red-labelled bottles in Chinatown. If you can't find it, replace it with equal parts dark soy sauce and Worcestershire sauce or with Bragg's liquid aminos.

In a large pitcher, combine the tomato juice, orange juice, lime juice, salt, pepper, onion powder, garlic powder, paprika, sherry vinegar, Tabasco and habanero sauce. Stir well. Chill in the refrigerator for several hours, or overnight. When ready to serve, strain through a very fine sieve.

In a shallow dish, combine the celery salt, taco seasoning mix and salt. Rub the rim of six tall glasses with a lime and twist the top of each glass through the salt blend. Pour 4 oz of tomato juice mixture and 4 oz of beer into each glass and stir. Add a dash of Maggi seasoning to each glass and fill to the top with ice. Garnish with pickled tomatillos or other pickled vegetables and lime wedges.

1 ¾ cups tomato juice
1 cup fresh orange juice
2 oz fresh lime juice
½ tsp sea salt
¼ tsp ground black pepper
¼ tsp onion powder
¼ tsp garlic powder
¼ tsp paprika
¼ oz sherry vinegar
¼ oz chipotle Tabasco
¼ oz habanero sauce
1 Tbsp celery salt
1 Tbsp taco seasoning mix
2 tsp sea salt
2 (each 12 oz) bottles of Mexican-style lager such as Vancouver Island Brewing Juan De Fuca Cerveza
Maggi seasoning sauce
Pickled tomatillos, asparagus or beans, for garnish
Lime wedges, for garnish

HIDE + SEEK COFFEE

When you walk into Hide + Seek Coffee, you are met with a delightful vibe: it's a bright and cheery little space full of people on their laptops, friends catching up, folks reading quietly and two dedicated owners who know their coffee. This is a place where all the little things that make a coffee shop unique and outstanding come together in one cool and cohesive spot. Grab a seat by the window to watch the goings-on of Oak Bay Village, listen as the turntable spins classic rock and new favourites, or pick up a magazine and settle in with a homemade treat and a latte. It would be easy to lounge and snack away the morning, but the day must go on. Make sure you grab a homemade pop tart on the way out (yes, you heard me right) and be sure to get back here on Sunday, early, before the waffles all sell out.

HIDE + SEEK COFFEE

2207

OAK BAY AVENUE

— hideandseekcoffee.ca →

778.265.0642

Honey-Orange Waffles with Candied Pecans

MAKES 12-15 WAFFLES

A delicious sweet treat to make at home, these waffles make for an impressive presentation. Though this recipe looks like a long one, the butter and pecans can be made well ahead. And if you happen to be wandering around Oak Bay Village on a Sunday morning, pop in to see what the waffle of the week is!

TO MAKE THE HONEY-ORANGE WHIPPED BUTTER

Whip the butter, zest and juice, and honey together in a stand mixer fitted with the paddle attachment, or in a bowl with a handheld mixer, for 5–10 minutes, until fluffy and well blended. It will keep in an airtight container in the refrigerator for up to 5 days. Remove from the refrigerator at least ½ hour before using.

TO MAKE THE CANDIED PECANS

Preheat the oven to 250°F. Line a baking sheet with parchment paper.
In a small bowl, mix together the sugar, cinnamon and salt. Set aside.
In another small bowl, whisk the egg white until frothy but not stiff. Toss in the pecans and stir well. Add the sugar mixture, then the maple syrup, and toss until evenly coated.

Spread the pecans evenly on the prepared baking sheet, and bake for 45 minutes, stirring occasionally so they brown evenly throughout. Remove from the oven and let cool.

Once cooled, pulse them in a food processor or chop with a large chef's knife until they are broken up, but not too small.

TO MAKE THE HONEY WHIPPED CREAM

In a stand mixer fitted with the whisk attachment, or in a bowl with a handheld mixer, whip the cream until stiff peaks form. With the mixer running, slowly drizzle in the honey until well blended. This will keep in an airtight container in the refrigerator for up to 2 days.

TO MAKE THE WAFFLES

Preheat the waffle iron to medium-high. Preheat the oven to 200°F.
In a large bowl, mix together the flour, baking powder, baking soda and salt.
In a medium bowl, whisk by hand the egg yolks with the melted butter and sugar. Add the vanilla bean seeds (or extract) and whisk until incorporated.
Whisk in the buttermilk and cream until completely smooth.

Honey-Orange Whipped Butter
½ cup salted butter,
    at room temperature
Zest and juice of ½ large orange
3 Tbsp honey

Candied Pecans
¼ cup granulated sugar
2 tsp ground cinnamon
½ tsp kosher salt
1 egg white
1 ½ cups pecan halves
1 Tbsp maple syrup

Honey Whipped Cream
2 cups whipping (35%) cream
¼ cup honey

Waffles
3 ½ cups all-purpose flour
3 tsp baking powder
2 tsp baking soda
1 tsp kosher salt
6 large eggs, separated
1 cup salted butter, melted,
    cooled slightly
1 cup granulated sugar
1 vanilla bean, seeds scraped,
    or 1 tsp pure vanilla extract
3 cups buttermilk
½ cup whipping (35%) cream
Grated orange zest, for garnish

Pour the wet ingredients into the dry, and whisk until smooth. Do not overmix. A few lumps are okay.

In a stand mixer fitted with the whisk attachment, or in a bowl with a handheld mixer, whip the egg whites for 5–7 minutes, until soft peaks form. Using a spatula, fold the egg whites into the batter. (At this point, the batter can be stored in an airtight container in the refrigerator for up to 2 days.)

Pour ½–¾ cup of batter (depending on the size and shape of your waffle iron) into the centre of the heated waffle iron. Close the lid and cook until golden brown and crisp. Repeat with the remaining batter. Keep the cooked waffles warm in the oven.

TO ASSEMBLE

Place the desired number of waffles on warm plates. Top with honey-orange butter, honey whipped cream and candied pecans. Garnish with grated orange zest.

THE HOT AND COLD CAFÉ

Did I mention that I have a soft spot for small, intimate spaces with super homemade food? Here's another. The Hot and Cold Café is a sweet little joint found in the heart of Cook Street Village, with an ever-changing menu and beautiful locally sourced ingredients. And it's run by some great folks who love their work and care about what they feed you! You'll experience a warm and inviting, homey sort of feel as you tuck yourself into a window seat or hang out on their sidewalk patio. Grab a giant latte, savour whatever it is they have cooking for brunch and walk it all off afterwards with a stroll around the village or a visit to Beacon Hill Park.

THE HOT AND COLD CAFÉ

1-313
COOK STREET
— thehotandcoldcafe.com →
778.433.1007

THE HOT AND COLD CAFÉ

Roasted Veggie Brunch Bowl

This is a very versatile dish—you could add or substitute whatever veggies you have in your refrigerator (or your garden) to this brunch bowl. Prefer fried eggs? Go for it. Have an abundance of oregano? Add that instead of basil. Just don't skip the Goddess Tahini dressing.

TO MAKE THE VEGGIES

Preheat the oven to 425°F.

In a large bowl, toss the potatoes and onions with 2 Tbsp of the olive oil and the oregano to coat, and season to taste with salt and pepper. Pour them into a roasting pan, making sure the pieces are evenly spaced and not too crowded. Roast in the oven for 8–10 minutes, or until the potatoes are just starting to get tender. Using the same bowl (no need to wipe it out), combine the carrots, yam, bell pepper, ginger, garlic, coriander, cumin and remaining 2 Tbsp olive oil. Season to taste with salt and pepper. Add these to the potatoes in the roasting pan and roast for another 15–20 minutes, stirring occasionally so they roast evenly. When the potatoes and yams are cooked, remove the pan from the oven, add the capers and basil and toss with a spatula to combine. Turn the oven off and keep the pan in the oven until ready to serve.

TO MAKE THE GODDESS TAHINI DRESSING

Place the tahini, vinegar, nutritional yeast, garlic, flax oil, hemp oil (or olive oil), oregano, basil, salt, pepper and about 1/3 cup water in a blender. Blend at high speed until well mixed, smooth and creamy. Add more water, about 1 Tbsp at a time, as necessary and continue to blend until dressing is the desired consistency. This will keep in an airtight container in the refrigerator for up to 3 days.

TO ASSEMBLE

Poach the eggs. (See page 183.)

Divide the potato mixture evenly between four shallow bowls. Tuck some fresh greens in on the side. Top each bowl with two poached eggs and garnish with fresh basil. Serve with Goddess Tahini dressing.

Veggies

2 large red potatoes, skins on, cut into 1-inch dice
1 red onion, julienned
4 Tbsp olive oil, divided
1 Tbsp dried oregano
Salt and ground black pepper
2 medium carrots, cut into 1-inch dice
1 large yam, skin on, cut into 1-inch dice
1 small red bell pepper, cut into 1-inch dice
1 Tbsp finely minced ginger
1 Tbsp finely minced garlic
1 tsp ground coriander
1 tsp ground cumin
1 Tbsp capers
¼ cup loosely packed fresh basil, julienned

Goddess Tahini Dressing

½ cup tahini
¼ cup apple cider vinegar
½ cup nutritional yeast
2 tsp finely minced garlic
1½ tsp flax oil
1½ tsp hemp oil
½ tsp dried oregano
½ tsp dried basil (or 1 Tbsp fresh)
½ tsp kosher salt
¼ tsp fresh ground black pepper

To assemble

8 eggs
1 cup fresh julienned greens (lettuce, kale, chard)
Fresh basil sprigs, for garnish

HUDSON'S ON FIRST

As dedicated Islanders, we are often travelling up-island. Whether for a camp or a hike in beautiful Parksville, a trip to breathtaking Tofino or just a no-reason roadie, it is always good to have "that favourite spot" to stop at. Somewhere in the heart of the Cowichan Valley feels about right. I'd heard a lot about Hudson's on First from various sources describing their incredible food and ambiance.

When I first stepped into Hudson's, I fell in love at first sight with the beautiful space. The stunning, but unpretentious old-house turned new is truly magnificent. I love old converted homes, and the detail and style of this one make it lovely and inviting. A porch-front brunch or dinner in one of their fine rooms is the perfect addition to any road trip, whichever direction you're travelling in.

HUDSON'S ON FIRST

163
FIRST ST., DUNCAN BC

→ hudsonsonfirst.ca →

250.597.0066

I have a strong draw to the Cowichan Valley. Filled with countless vineyards and wineries, old barns, antique shops and other hidden gems of all sorts, it is a place I love for all its diversity. I drive through it often, whether en route to somewhere far or to a local destination, and it makes me happy every time. Check out the winery tours or the shops in Cowichan Bay, or just drive around, meandering through winding roads, waving to the cows in the fields.

Salt Spring Island Mussels with House-made Sausage

> Mussels and sausage are a fantastic combination, especially when you use this absolutely delicious house-made sausage. Serve this with the traditional frites or a nice crusty loaf as part of a West Coast brunch. (If you don't have a meat grinder, substitute the pork meat and fat with about 4 lb pork sausage.)

TO MAKE THE SAUSAGE

If using whole pork, cut the meat and fat into ½-inch chunks and pass them through the coarse blade of a meat grinder. Alternatively, chop the pork into small dice and place it in the freezer on a large plate for 15 minutes. Remove from the freezer and pulse in a food processor, with the pork fat, fitted with the steel blade until the meat has a ground texture. Do not overmix as the meat will get gummy.

In a large bowl, and using a wooden spoon, mix together the ground meat, garlic, salt, paprika, pepper, thyme, ground bay leaf and fennel seed. Form a bite-sized patty and cook it in the frying pan to taste. Adjust the seasonings if necessary. Form the rest of the meat into roughly bite-sized clusters.

Heat a small frying pan over medium-high heat and add the oil. Sear the pork until cooked through and slightly browned, stirring occasionally. Set aside.

TO MAKE THE MUSSELS

Place a large pot over medium-high heat. Add the butter and oil, and then the shallots and garlic. Cook, stirring constantly, for 5–7 minutes, until the shallots are transparent and just starting to colour. Add the white wine and lemon juice. Add the mussels and toss to coat evenly. Cover and let cook for about 5 minutes, until the mussels have opened (discard any mussels that don't open). Add the cream, salt and cooked pork (you may not use all of the sausage) and heat through for 2 minutes. Using a slotted spoon, dish out all the opened mussels into a shallow bowl, leaving the sauce in the pot. Turn the stove to high and add the tomatoes to the sauce. As soon as the sauce is hot, but just before it boils (you'll need to give this your full attention), remove from the heat, taste and adjust the amount of lemon juice or salt to taste. Pour the sauce over the mussels and garnish with parsley and espelette pepper.

Sausage
4 lb lean pork meat
2 lb pork fat
¼ cup minced garlic
2 Tbsp coarse kosher salt
1 Tbsp paprika
1 tsp ground black pepper
¼ tsp dried thyme
¼ tsp ground bay leaf
¼ tsp ground fennel seed
2 tsp vegetable oil

Mussels
2 Tbsp unsalted butter
2 tsp olive oil
2 medium shallots, thinly sliced
2 garlic cloves, thinly sliced
½ cup dry white wine
2 tsp fresh lemon juice
2 lb Salt Spring Island mussels, cleaned and de-bearded
⅔ cup whipping (35%) cream
Pinch of kosher salt
½ cup cherry tomatoes, cut in half
2 Tbsp chopped flat-leaf or curly parsley
Pinch of ground espelette pepper (or paprika)

Hudson's on First Corpse Reviver #2

SERVES 2

A Corpse Reviver #2 is one of my favourite cocktails. Vancouver Island's Ampersand brand is the perfect gin to complement the absinthe and lemon.

Splash of absinthe
2 oz London dry gin
2 oz Cointreau
2 oz Lillet
2 oz fresh lemon juice
Ice cubes
2 wide lemon zest curls

In two chilled martini glasses, swirl a splash of absinthe around to coat the glass then discard any excess absinthe. To a Boston shaker, add the gin, Cointreau, Lillet, lemon juice and ice cubes. Shake vigorously and strain into the martini glasses. Garnish each with a lemon curl.

JAM CAFÉ

Oh, Jam. You swooped into town and took over breakfast. With an astonishingly large fan base right from the beginning, there is inevitably a lineup at your door at 2:00 pm on a Wednesday. And 9:00 am on a Tuesday. And it goes without saying that your weekends are madness. And no wonder. Pulled pork pancakes. Brioche French toast. Fried chicken benedict. Is that it? Or is it your super-hip Portland-esque interior? Your huge portions? Awesome music? We all know that if we're hungry and want something satisfying that will help us last until dinnertime, and we want to be part of a fun, happening crowd, we should go to Jam. You're sort of old-town. Homemade. Rustic with an upbeat ambience. With inviting, friendly staff and a penchant for great drinks and a killer vibe. You've got it all. Nice work, Jam. We are in love.

JAM CAFÉ

542
HERALD STREET
jamcafes.com
778.440.4489

Pulled Pork Pancakes

SERVES 4

Jam has given us the gift of a grand dish here. It's long, yes, with several steps, but don't let that scare you. Making extra pulled pork and stashing some in the freezer is always a good option. After all, you'll likely need it next weekend. If this is more of a spontaneous craving you can always purchase some of your favourite pulled pork instead.

TO MAKE THE BRINE

In a large stockpot over high heat, bring the water, salt, onion powder and garlic powder to a boil. Remove from the heat and allow to cool completely.

TO MAKE THE DRY RUB

Combine the brown sugar, regular paprika, smoked paprika, thyme, cayenne pepper, onion powder, garlic powder and black pepper in a bowl. Set aside.

TO MAKE THE PORK

Place the pork in the large stockpot of cooled brine and refrigerate overnight. Remove from the refrigerator about ½ hour before you are ready to roast.

Preheat the oven to 450°F.

Remove the pork from the brine and pat it dry with paper towels. Place it in a large roasting pan, making sure there is a little space around it. Rub the pork with the dry rub, massaging it well into all the cracks and crevices. Roast in the oven, uncovered, for about 30 minutes, until the butt starts to brown on the outside.

Remove the pork from the oven and turn down the oven temperature to 275°F.

Combine the chipotle paste with the water and smother it over the pork. Add the pineapple, garlic and coriander to the roasting pan, arranging it around the roast. Pour in the apple juice around the roast and cover tightly with aluminum foil. Return to the oven and roast for about 12 hours. Remove from the oven and let cool. Once cooled, shred the pork apart with two forks, removing any large pieces of fat, and set aside. (You may have more pork than you will need for this recipe. Extras can be kept in an airtight container in the refrigerator for 4 days or frozen for up to 3 months.)

TO MAKE THE MAPLE BOURBON BBQ GLAZE

In a medium bowl, combine the BBQ sauce, maple syrup and bourbon. Mix well, cover tightly and refrigerate for up to 3 days.

Brine

6 cups water
½ cup coarse salt
2 tsp onion powder
2 tsp garlic powder

Dry Rub

¼ cup brown sugar, packed
2 Tbsp regular paprika
1 ½ tsp smoked paprika
1 ½ tsp dried thyme
1 ½ tsp cayenne pepper
1 ½ tsp onion powder
1 ½ tsp garlic powder
1 ½ tsp ground black pepper

Pork

6 lb pork butt
¼ cup chipotle paste
2 Tbsp water
¼ pineapple, chopped
8 garlic cloves, smashed
1 ½ tsp coriander seeds
3 cups apple juice

Maple Bourbon BBQ Glaze

1 cup of your favourite
    BBQ sauce
1 cup maple syrup (any grade
    except pancake syrup)
2 Tbsp of your favourite bourbon

Jalapeño Sour Cream

1 cup full-fat sour cream
1 Tbsp fresh lime juice
½ bunch of cilantro, finely minced
1 garlic clove, minced

TO MAKE THE JALAPEÑO SOUR CREAM

In a small bowl, combine the sour cream and lime juice with the cilantro, garlic, jalapeño and salt. Mix well, cover tightly and refrigerate for up to 2 days.

TO MAKE THE PANCAKES

Preheat the oven to 200°F.

Place the egg whites in the bowl of a stand mixer fitted with the whisk attachment and whip on high speed for about 5 minutes, until stiff peaks form.

In a medium bowl, combine the egg yolks, milk and vanilla. In a large bowl, whisk the flour, baking powder and salt with the sugar. Slowly add the wet ingredients to the dry ingredients. Do not overmix—it should still be a little lumpy. Gently fold in half the egg whites, then carefully fold in the other half. Do not overmix, or the whites will collapse.

Heat about 1 Tbsp oil in a large cast iron griddle or frying pan over medium-high heat. Using a ladle, add some batter to the pan. Your pancakes should be 6–8 inches in diameter. You will need eight pancakes. Cook for about 4 minutes, until golden brown and the surface bubbles begin to pop. Flip and cook the other side until golden brown, about 2 minutes. Keep the cooked pancakes warm in the oven until you're ready to serve.

TO ASSEMBLE

Place a pancake on a serving plate and top with about ¼ cup of pulled pork and 2 Tbsp BBQ glaze. Place a second pancake on top, and top that one with even more pulled pork, more BBQ glaze, plus some jalapeño sour cream, diced tomatoes, chopped scallions, and fresh cilantro. Serve immediately.

1 tsp fresh jalapeño pepper, finely minced
Pinch of kosher salt

Pancakes
6 eggs, separated
3 cups whole milk
1 tsp pure vanilla extract
3 cups all-purpose flour
2 Tbsp baking powder
Pinch of kosher salt
¾ cup granulated sugar
Grapeseed or canola oil, for frying

To assemble
2 Roma tomatoes, diced
4 scallions, chopped
Fresh cilantro, for garnish

THE MARINA RESTAURANT

The Marina Restaurant is a hidden gem, just a little outside of town, in Oak Bay. Trust me when I say that the extra 10-minute drive (or 30-minute bike ride) is worth it. The culinary team there is mega-talented, offering fresh, local and house-made ingredients and the best 100% Ocean Wise seafood they can get their hands on. Their love of beautiful food is apparent in their plating, and I have always admired their dedication to sustainability and quality. They serve a wicked brunch, but really, they're worth a visit any time.

The Marina Restaurant perches on the edge of a gorgeous marina with an ocean view, and provides you with one of the only remaining brunch buffets in town. They have all the usual suspects—bennies, pancakes, French toast, scrambled eggs, bacon and sausages—as well as such savouries as curried chicken, sushi and smoked fish, pasta and an array of salads. And desserts. And brunchy drinks. Clear your Sunday calendar and wear your elastic-waist pants. This could take all day.

After brunch, head down to the docks at the marina to visit with the resident seals. Grab a coffee at the Marina Eatery, then have a wander down Beach Ave. in either direction. Oak Bay has a lot to offer, from its main drag on Oak Bay Ave., to Estevan Village, to a walk along Willows Beach. When you're done with all that, return to The Marina for some of the best sushi around.

THE MARINA RESTAURANT

1327 BEACH DRIVE

— marinarestaurant.com →

250.598.8555

Marina Brioche Cinnamon Buns

MAKES 24

> Ah, these cinnamon buns are to die for. They are the epitome of the gooey, sweet but not too sugary, beautifully raised buns that make you close your eyes when you eat one. Or two. This recipe makes a lot, but don't worry—they'll be gone before you know it.
>
> This recipe can be made by hand or in a mixer with the hook attachment.

TO MAKE THE SPONGE

Place the flour and yeast in a large bowl (or in the bowl of a stand mixer). The milk should be between 89°F–100°F. Stir in the milk until fully combined. Cover the bowl with plastic wrap and let sit on the counter for 30–45 minutes, or until the sponge rises and falls when you tap the bowl.

TO MAKE THE DOUGH

Add the eggs to the sponge and whisk until smooth. In a separate bowl, stir together the flour, sugar and salt. Add this to the sponge and mix until all the ingredients are fully combined and there are no dry spots or chunks. Cover loosely with a clean dish towel and let the mixture rest in the bowl on the counter for 5–10 minutes. Turn the dough out onto a lightly floured surface and, with clean hands, gradually mix in the ¾ cup of butter about 1 Tbsp at a time, fully incorporating each addition before adding more.

Continue kneading dough for about 10 minutes more, until the dough is very smooth and soft and not too sticky too handle. Add a small amount of flour if the dough is too sticky. Drape a clean tea towel over the dough and let it rest on the counter for 10–15 minutes.

TO MAKE THE CINNAMON SUGAR

While the dough is resting, mix together the granulated sugar, brown sugar and cinnamon in a medium bowl. Set aside.

TO MAKE THE SUGAR BASE

In a medium bowl and using a hand mixer, or in the bowl of a stand mixer fitted with the paddle attachment, cream together the butter, both sugars, corn syrup, vanilla and salt for about 5 minutes, until light and fluffy. Divide the sugar base between two 8-inch square pans, spreading the base evenly and loosely across the bottom of both pans.

Sponge

¾ cup unbleached bread flour
1 Tbsp instant yeast
¾ cup whole milk, lukewarm

Dough

6 large eggs, lightly beaten
4¾ cups unbleached bread flour
3 Tbsp granulated sugar
1¾ tsp kosher salt
¾ cup unsalted butter, at room temperature
2 Tbsp unsalted butter

Cinnamon Sugar

1 cup granulated sugar
1 cup brown sugar, packed
1 Tbsp ground cinnamon

Sugar Base

1 cup unsalted butter, at room temperature
½ cup granulated sugar
½ cup brown sugar, packed
½ cup golden corn syrup
1 tsp pure vanilla extract
¼ tsp kosher salt

Cream Cheese Frosting

1¼ cups plain full-fat cream cheese, at room temperature
1 tsp pure vanilla extract
Seeds of 1 vanilla bean or ¼ tsp more vanilla extract
½ cup unsalted butter, at room temperature, cut into 1-inch pieces
2 cups icing sugar

TO BAKE

Melt the 2 Tbsp butter. Roll the dough out on a clean, lightly floured surface into a large rectangle, about ¼ inch thick. Brush it with the melted butter and sprinkle the cinnamon sugar mixture evenly overtop.

Starting at a long side, roll up the dough, firmly but not tightly, into an even log. Cut the log into 24 pieces.

Place the cinnamon buns, slightly spaced out, on top of the sugar mixture in both pans.

Cover the pans lightly with clean dish towels and let the cinnamon buns rise on the counter for about 45 minutes, until they are about double in size.

Preheat the oven to 350°F.

Bake the cinnamon buns for 20–30 minutes, until golden and fully baked. When a toothpick inserted into the doughy part of a bun comes out clean, remove the pans from the oven and set them on a wire rack to cool.

TO MAKE THE CREAM CHEESE FROSTING

While the buns are cooling, make the frosting.

Using a stand mixer fitted with the paddle attachment, or a bowl and a hand mixer on medium speed, beat the cream cheese, vanilla extract and vanilla bean seeds for about 3 minutes, until light and fluffy. Add the butter, one piece at a time and mixing well between additions, and continue to mix until well combined. Turn the speed of the mixer to low and add the icing sugar, 1 cup at a time, mixing well between additions. Continue beating until smooth and fluffy. The icing can be spread over warm or cooled cinnamon buns, or stored in an airtight container in the refrigerator for up to 3 days. Bring the icing to room temperature and beat until fluffy before spreading on the cinnamon buns.

MO:LÉ

When I first moved to Victoria in 2004, I found it a semi-challenging city to get to know, with lots of one-way streets that turn unexpectedly into two-way streets while at the same time changing names. Junctions and dead ends and little old-town alleyways abound, and sometimes I would get lost on purpose to see if I could figure out my way home. One day, during one of these exploration adventures, I happened upon a one-way street called Pandora (by way of Oak Bay and Fort St. and a junction or two, of course). At the end of it, down by the bridge, I came across the newly opened Mo:Lé, a little brick-walled and concrete-floored hole in the wall. I tried the Mo's Biscuit that day, and I have never looked back. That visit remains one of my fondest memories of my first months here, and even now, when I visit the bright little space, I get that sort of new hometown feeling. I don't think Mo:Lé is what made me stay in Victoria, but it sure didn't hurt.

The menu has a super variety of meat-lover, vegan and vegetarian dishes, including the fantastic vegetarian recipe they've shared with us here. With a conscious focus on healthy and delicious, good times and happy customers, Mo:Lé is one of Victoria's long-time greats, and I am sure it will remain so always.

Red Pepper Polenta with Eggs and Fruit Salsa

A healthy and delicious dish, this one is great to prepare ahead. The polenta can be made the day before, cooked and fried, then heated lightly in the oven just before serving.

TO MAKE THE RED PEPPER POLENTA

Lightly butter a 9-inch square baking pan.

Bring the water and wine to a boil in a large pot over high heat. Turn down the heat to a simmer, and stir in the polenta, salt and pepper. Cook, stirring almost constantly, for 10–15 minutes, or until the polenta is softened and thick. Remove from the heat. Stir in the bell pepper, both cheeses and the butter. Pour this into the prepared baking pan and give the pan a tap on the counter to even it out. It will firm up substantially as it cools. This can be made a day ahead and kept tightly wrapped in the refrigerator.

TO MAKE THE MANGO SALSA

Mix all the ingredients together in a small bowl. Season to taste with salt and pepper. This will keep in an airtight container in the refrigerator for up to 3 days.

TO ASSEMBLE

Preheat the oven to 200°F. Line a plate with paper towels. Line a sheet pan with parchment paper.

Cut the polenta into eight pieces. Heat 2 Tbsp vegetable oil in a frying pan over medium-high heat. Place four slices of polenta in the pan and cook for about 4 minutes, until brown and crispy. Flip and repeat on the other side. Remove from the pan and place on the prepared plate to absorb any excess oil. Then, transfer to the prepared sheet pan and place in the oven to keep warm. Repeat with the remaining pieces of polenta.

Poach the eggs. (See page 183.)

Place two pieces of warm polenta, side by side, on each of four plates. Top each with a slice of Havarti and two poached eggs. Lay a piece of roasted red pepper over the eggs and add some mango salsa and fresh cilantro. Season with salt and pepper and serve immediately.

Red Pepper Polenta
Butter for greasing pan
3½ cups water
½ cup dry white wine
1 cup polenta
1½ tsp kosher salt
½ tsp ground black pepper
¼ cup finely diced red bell pepper
¼ cup grated Parmesan cheese
¼ cup grated Havarti cheese
2 Tbsp butter

Mango Salsa
1 Ataulfo mango, very finely diced
½ small red onion, very finely diced
½ small white onion, very finely diced
½ red bell pepper, very finely diced
½ bunch of cilantro leaves, finely chopped
2 Tbsp fresh lemon juice
1 Tbsp fresh lime juice
Salt and ground black pepper

To assemble
Vegetable oil, for frying
8 eggs
4 thin slices of havarti cheese
4 large pieces of roasted red bell pepper, homemade or from a jar
8 sprigs of fresh cilantro
Salt and ground black pepper

BOYS *Who* BRUNCH

I am always interested in and curious about how a food joint gets established, and more importantly, stays established, in a restaurant-saturated town like Victoria. Josh Miller, owner and operator of Mo:Lé, has been making it work, and work well, for 13 years. In this town, that's saying something.

Josh was born and raised in Victoria, so he has seen the progress, growth and changes in our restaurant scene over the years. As a teenager in the early '90s, he enjoyed brunch as part of his regular weekend routine. "Brunch is the best because you can go dressed up. You can go hungover. You can go in your pajamas. It's casual. It's cost-effective. It's fully satisfying." In those days, unlike today when there are dozens of brunch places to choose from, Josh frequented one or two standard joints, such as the hippy-esque Prancing Pony in Fernwood or Goodies Restaurant on Broad St.

Josh got an early start at the age of 13, when he helped out at the Prancing Pony, where his dad was a server. One day, being the ever-resourceful entrepreneur, he asked for half of his dad's tips once the shift was over, joking that he was never asked back after that. A few years later, however, the Prancing Pony became the Soho Village Bistro, and Josh took on a job himself. He continued along this path into his early adulthood, learning at the hip of some of Victoria's best restaurateurs, before taking a side journey into a career in finance that ultimately brought him to where he is today.

In 2004, he opened the now well-known breakfast and lunch restaurant Mo:Lé with his friend and business partner, Cosmo Meens. (The name Mo:Lé is a combination of CosMO and LEah, Cosmo's wife. Josh kids that he is represented by the colon in the middle.)

While Cosmo is no longer a part of Mo:Lé, Josh has managed to make an institution of it. It is clear from talking with him that his desire to create an outstanding experience for his guests is his priority. This is not only a wise business move, but also truly in Josh's nature. I can see this in his body language, as he animatedly reflects on the years he's been running the restaurant, greeting guests and running

food in the dining room five to six days per week. "Treat breakfast like dinner. Give them a great product that is visually appealing and worthy of the money they spend. Treat each guest like your own grandmother, and put all the love into it."

Like anyone who takes on a massive life-changing project, Josh has learned along the way. Managing a staff and running a business is not easy, but he seems to be doing something right. Many of the restaurant staff have been there for a long time, which is always a sign of a well-run establishment, and it's fun to be greeted by their familiar faces.

Most things you eat at Mo:Lé are house-made. And if they're not, they are from one of the many local suppliers on Vancouver Island or close by, such as Galloping Goose sausages and Salt Spring sprouts. The meals are healthful, beautiful and consistently delicious. The same menu is available at Mo:Lé's new location in Langford, which opened in March 2017. In each location, you can build your own breakfast with such things as mushroom house-made sausage, grilled tomatoes and a vegan tofu scramble. Go for something sweet, like the house-made vanilla granola or Life of Rhiely Griddle Cakes. Choose from scrambles, bennies, omelettes or any of Mo:Lé's classics, such as Mo's Biscuit. Any way you go with this, you can be sure that it will be delicious and satisfying, in all the best ways.

NORTHERN QUARTER

Northern Quarter, fondly known as NQ, is a vibrant, welcoming, casual and comfortable place, with a sort of modern-day supper-club feel. Think wonderful food and drinks paired with comedy shows, quiz nights, and live music, giving the space an eclectic and quirky vibe.

One half of the NQ talent is Benji Duke (right) of Fort Street Café fame. The other half is Torin Egan (left), who used to be the chef at the Superior Café. Bringing the skills and creativity of these two together was a no-brainer.

Lisa Boehme, the owner of the Superior Café, lived above her restaurant, and on weekends she always requested her special order: pancakes with bacon, scrambled eggs, and maple syrup. Soon, customers began asking her what she was eating and ordering it themselves. Eventually, it showed up on the menu.

When Torin and Benji opened NQ, Torin re-envisioned the recipe for his own menu. He added peppery greens, crispy confit pork belly, and poached eggs instead of scrambled. Lisa left BC when the Superior closed, and this recipe is Torin's tribute to her. We all hope to lure her back with this version of her infamous breakfast.

NORTHERN QUARTER

1724
DOUGLAS STREET

→ northernquarter.ca →

250.590.7702

THE NQ Breakfast

If the prospect of curing, braising and cooking pork belly intimidates you, don't despair. Grab some extra-thick cut bacon from one of our local butchers and cook that up instead. Or better yet, pop into Northern Quarter one weekend and let them do the cooking.

TO MAKE THE PORK BELLY

Lay the pork belly on a plate and rub it all over with the sugar, salt and pepper. Place it in the refrigerator, covered, for at least 2 hours, and up to 10 hours.

Preheat the oven to 300°F.

Choose an ovenproof dish with a lid that is only slightly larger than the pork belly, but large enough that the pork will be surrounded by the fat. Put the belly in the pot and pour the fat over it. The fat should cover the pork by ½– ¾ inches. Cover and cook for 2 ½–3 hours, or until completely tender. Let cool.

Carefully remove the belly from the fat and press it between two plates, setting a can or something heavy on top to weigh it down. Refrigerate for a minimum of 4 hours, or up to overnight.

Heat a heavy frying pan over high heat. Line a plate with paper towel. Cut the belly into eight strips and sear for about 4 minutes per side, until crisp. Transfer to the prepared plate to soak up any excess fat.

TO MAKE THE PANCAKES

Sift the flour, sugar, baking powder, baking soda and salt into a large bowl. In another bowl, combine the egg yolks, buttermilk and melted butter. Carefully stir this wet mixture into the dry mixture, being careful not to overmix (a few lumps are okay).

Using a hand mixer or a stand mixer fitted with the whipping attachment, whip the egg whites to soft peaks and gently fold them into the batter.

Preheat the oven to 400°F. Grease an 8-inch non-stick frying pan or cast iron pan with butter.

Pour about 1 cup (you will need four pancakes) of batter into the prepared pan and place it in the oven. Cook for 5 minutes and flip. Cook for another 5 minutes. Test for doneness by inserting a toothpick into the centre of the pancake. If it comes out clean, it is cooked. If it is coated with batter, pop the pan back in the oven for another 2–3 minutes. If you have more than one frying pan, use them simultaneously to speed up the process. While you are cooking each pancake, keep the cooked ones on a plate at the back of the stove and cover them with foil to keep warm.

Pork belly

1 lb fresh pork belly
¼ cup granulated sugar
¼ cup kosher salt
1 tsp ground black pepper
2½ lb rendered fat (lard, bacon fat, duck fat, or in a pinch, vegetable oil)

Pancakes

2½ cups all-purpose flour
⅓ cup granulated sugar
1 Tbsp baking powder
1½ tsp baking soda
1 tsp kosher salt
3 eggs, separated
3 cups buttermilk
3 Tbsp melted unsalted butter, cooled
Butter for greasing pan

Maple Whiskey Syrup

1 cup maple syrup (any grade except pancake syrup)
2 oz whiskey
½ tsp ground black pepper

To assemble

8 large eggs
Extra virgin olive oil
Salt and ground black pepper
Pea shoots or other delicate greens

TO MAKE THE MAPLE WHISKEY SYRUP

In a small pan over low heat, combine the syrup, whiskey and black pepper. Stirring, bring it to a low simmer. Turn the heat off and cover the pan to keep warm.

TO ASSEMBLE

Poach the eggs. (See page 183.)

Place a cooked pancake on each of four warm plates. Top each one with two pieces of pork belly and douse with some of the warm maple syrup. Top with two poached eggs. Drizzle the eggs with a little olive oil, season to taste with salt and pepper and top with a sprinkling of pea shoots.

NORTHERN QUARTER

Northern Quarter's Breakfast Uppercut

MAKES 1 COCKTAIL

NQ uses Vancouver Island's de Vine New Tom Gin for this refreshing mid-morning cocktail.

In a 10 oz glass filled with ice cubes, pour the gin, syrup, San Pellegrino and lemon juice. Garnish with a lemon wheel and mint sprig.

2 oz barrel-aged gin
2 oz Earl Grey and mint tea syrup (see below)
1 ½ oz San Pellegrino Limonata or other carbonated lemon drink
½ oz fresh lemon juice
Lemon wheel and mint sprig, for garnish

Earl Grey and Mint Tea Syrup

Northern Quarter uses Earth's Herbal Earl Grey and Earth's Herbal Happy Tea by Lily Fawn.

Bring the water and sugar to a simmer in a small pot over medium-high heat and allow to simmer, stirring, for about 2 minutes, until the sugar has dissolved. Remove from the heat and add both teas. Steep for 10 minutes, stir, then strain and chill.

This will keep in an airtight container in the refrigerator for several weeks.

MAKES 2 CUPS
2 cups water
½ cup granulated sugar
2 tsp Earl Grey loose tea
½ tsp mint loose tea

NOURISH KITCHEN AND CAFÉ

Nourish Kitchen and Café lives in a beautiful 1889 heritage home in James Bay with a lovely bright main dining room furnished with a fantastic array of mismatched tables and chairs and an eclectic collection of dishes. This is where you go when you want to keep your virtue in check, though judging by the taste of the food, you would never know it. Creamy cashew hollandaise, pancakes unlike any you've ever tried, and Five Mushroom Drinking Chocolate—magic in its own way.

The café space in the house is where you can grab some bone broth to go, baked goods, house-made water kefir or anything that is offered on the menu. Have some work to do? Head upstairs to the second floor, where you can hang out in the study or the parlour. If you have a little party to host, or want to organize a gathering of any sort, these rooms can be rented. You'll often find folks milling about these rooms during one of Nourish's many community events.

Nourish is a huge supporter of local goods, and it regularly uses such items as Silk Road Tea, Fantastico Coffee and a number of local Vancouver Island spirits. With a focus on health in body, mind and spirit, this sweet little space is definitely one to visit.

NOURISH KITCHEN AND CAFE

225 QUEBEC STREET

nourishkitchen.ca →

250.590.3426

Red Lentil Hummus

This is a super-simple take on a classic hummus with a really nice variation of texture, colour and nutrition. Here you see it topped with roasted shallots, scrambled eggs, butternut squash and arugula and served with seedy toast, which you can buy right at Nourish. It's a satisfying way to get some nutrient-rich carbs and proteins into your belly.

1 Tbsp + 1 tsp sea salt
1 cup + 2 Tbsp split red lentils
¼ cup creamy tahini
1 large garlic clove, roughly chopped
⅓ cup fresh lemon juice (1–2 lemons)
Zest of 1 lemon
½ cup extra virgin olive oil

Bring a large pot of water to a boil over high heat and add the 1 Tbsp sea salt.

Add the lentils to the boiling water, turn the heat down to medium and simmer, uncovered, for 5–7 minutes, until very soft.

Drain the lentils, reserving ½ cup of the cooking liquid, and let cool slightly.

In a food processor fitted with the steel blade, or in a blender, place the lentils, tahini, garlic, lemon juice and lemon zest. Pulse all the ingredients until lightly blended. Add all of the olive oil and the 1 tsp sea salt and blend on high speed until smooth, adding the reserved cooking liquid as needed to achieve the desired consistency.

Season with extra salt and lemon if desired. This can be stored in an airtight container in the refrigerator for up to 4 days.

You will know your lentils are done when they start to lose their colour. Red lentils typically lose all of their orange hue when cooked and turn a more beige colour. Once you see this happen, the lentils are ready. Take care to not overcook them!

While in James Bay, don't forget to check out Fisherman's Wharf. The little seaside collection of shops, restaurants and floating homes is a great place to hang out for the afternoon, followed by a stroll down magnificent Dallas Rd.

OLO

I first met Brad Holmes and his lovely wife, Sahara, in 2010 when they opened Ulla, a bright and unique restaurant in Victoria's Chinatown. Ulla was clearly ahead of its time (here in little Victoria, at least) in ambiance and food alike, and I vividly recall the first mind-blowing flavours I tasted from his unconventional menu. I have a clear recollection of Brad recounting to me a story about some basil-fed snails that he had been working with. Basil. Fed. Snails. I may not have heard anything after that, but I did know that this was a place I'd be returning to.

I came to recognize Brad's devotion to his craft, staying true to his training and not straying from his commitment to using real, high-quality ingredients. He is truly a passionate chef—and any conversation with him will confirm this.

After a few years, Brad and his team morphed Ulla into Olo. With a local, organic, farm-to-table focus and a super-flexible menu that follows the seasons and what is available locally, Olo still delivers like nowhere else.

One of the things I like best about Olo is that while Brad and his crew can create complex and layered dishes that make you wonder what sort of magic they've performed in the kitchen, they also take the simplest ingredients and elevate them to a new level. When you go there, make sure you leave yourself enough time to savour it all, course by course, cocktail by cocktail.

OLO RESTAURANT

509 FISGARD STREET

olorestaurant.com →

250.590.8795

Brunch Fried Rice

> I can't even pretend that we could get close to creating the dishes that Brad does, and even though this is his recipe, you are fully encouraged to make it your own. In any case, this dish is outstanding, with layers of flavours and textures. You must make the rice the day before and leave it uncovered in the refrigerator overnight. If you are not into fermenting your own vegetables, find yourself a quality jar of kimchi, sauerkraut, or other fermented or pickled vegetables. And if you are into it, I highly recommend grabbing any books on fermentation by Sandor Ellix Katz. He is the first and foremost authority on the subject, and if you go for it, you won't be sorry.

TO MAKE THE PICKLED GREEN GARLIC

Place the vinegar, cardamom pods, sugar, juniper berries, mustard seeds, ginger, fennel seed, coriander and red pepper flakes in a medium pot. Bring to a boil over high heat and cook for about 2 minutes, until the sugar has dissolved. Remove from the heat and let cool to room temperature.

Place the green garlic in a jar large enough to hold the garlic and the liquid. Pour the cooled liquid overtop, cover with a lid and refrigerate until ready to use. Extra garlic can be kept in its liquid in the refrigerator for several weeks.

TO MAKE THE GREEN GARLIC MAYONNAISE

Combine the mayonnaise, green garlic and pickle juice in a small bowl. Season to taste with salt and pepper. Set aside. If you don't use all of the mayonnaise, leftovers can be kept in an airtight container in the refrigerator for up to 3 days.

TO MAKE THE VINEGAR-PICKLED ONIONS

Place the onions, vinegar, salt and pepper in a small bowl and let sit for at least 10 minutes. If you don't use all of the onions for this recipe, leftovers can be stored in an airtight container in the refrigerator for up to 3 weeks.

TO MAKE THE FISH SAUCE

In a large measuring cup, combine the fish sauce, rice vinegar, chili garlic paste, sesame oil, tamari and fresh ginger.

TO MAKE THE FRIED RICE

Heat the oil in a large frying pan or wok over high heat until the oil begins to shimmer. Add the rice and cook until it is a bit crispy in parts. Add the garlic and

Pickled Green Garlic

2 cups apple cider vinegar
3 green cardamom pods, bruised
1 Tbsp granulated sugar
1 tsp juniper berries
1 tsp yellow or black mustard seeds
1 tsp chopped fresh ginger
1 tsp fennel seed
1 tsp coriander seeds
½ tsp crushed red pepper flakes
12 green garlic stalks, sliced into
   ½-inch rounds, white and light
   green parts only

Green Garlic Mayonnaise

4 Tbsp mayonnaise or aioli
2 tsp pickled green garlic,
   finely chopped
1 tsp green garlic pickle juice
Salt and ground black pepper

Vinegar-Pickled Onions

2 large red cipollini onions,
   sliced very thin
¼ cup apple cider vinegar
1 tsp kosher salt
Ground black pepper

Fish Sauce

¼ cup fish sauce
¼ cup rice vinegar
1 Tbsp chili garlic paste
1 tsp toasted sesame oil
1 tsp tamari
1 Tbsp fresh ginger, finely chopped

Fried Rice

¼ cup vegetable oil

cook for about 2 minutes, until it is softened. Transfer the rice and garlic to a large bowl and set aside.

Add the onion to the pan (plus more oil, if necessary) and cook, stirring constantly, for about 3 minutes, until the onion is softened. Add the cabbage and broccoli and continue to stir-fry over high heat for about 3 minutes, until the vegetables are slightly softened but still a bit crispy. Return the rice to the pan and mix in well with the vegetables.

Turn down the heat to low, and add the vinegar mixture to the pan, stirring well to combine all the ingredients. Add more vinegar, fish sauce or chili garlic paste, according to taste, if needed. Turn the stove off and cover the pan loosely with aluminum foil, leaving it vented, to keep warm. Do not continue to cook after the vinegar mixture has been added, or it will lose its flavour.

TO ASSEMBLE

Poach the eggs. (See page 183.)

Divide the rice evenly between four warm bowls. Top with the pickled onion, fermented vegetables, toasted pumpkin seeds, radishes, bacon (if using), scallions and a poached egg. Add a dollop of green garlic mayo.

This dish works great with any additional protein: leftover roasted chicken, pork belly or anything else!

5 cups day-old cooked
   short-grain brown rice
1 large garlic clove, minced
1 yellow onion, diced
½ small head green cabbage,
   finely shredded with a knife
   or mandoline
2 cups broccoli, cut into small florets

To assemble
4 large eggs
About ¾ cup lacto-fermented
   cabbage or kimchi or other
   fermented vegetables
3 Tbsp toasted pumpkin seeds
2 radishes, sliced very thin with a
   knife or mandoline
4 strips cooked thick-cut bacon or
   pork belly, chopped (optional)
3 scallions, chopped

Green garlic is the young garlic plant and is harvested in spring, before the garlic cloves have matured. Green garlic looks almost identical to a scallion (or green onion), except that its leaves are flat instead of tubular, and certain varieties have a pink hue over the white part of the little bulb. If you can't find green garlic, substitute scallions, garlic scapes or leeks in this recipe. When I made it, I used bunching onions from my garden and added a garlic clove to the pickling brine. No complaints.

Olo's Wake Up in the Dark

This iced coffee cocktail created jointly by the Olo bar team is perfect for getting the weekend started. Feel free to use what you have on hand, but Olo recommends Dark Horse Canadian rye whisky, Legend Distilling Blasted Brew coffee liqueur from BC's own Okanagan, Bows & Arrows coffee and Vancouver's Bittered Sling chocolate bitters.

2 oz Canadian rye whisky
1 oz coffee liqueur
2 oz fresh brewed espresso
2 dashes of chocolate bitters
Ice cubes
6 coffee beans, for garnish

Add the whisky, liqueur, espresso, chocolate bitters and ice cubes to a cocktail shaker and shake hard. Strain into two fancy glasses and garnish each one with three coffee beans.

PART + PARCEL

Some might challenge the designation of Part + Parcel as a "brunch place," but as I often find myself there around 11.30 am, I feel it deserves a mention.

This little place holds a special place in my heart for many reasons. It's partly due to Anna and Grant, who run the place and who are wildly open and down-to-earth and dedicated to their craft. It's also due to their special and amazing food, which is among the very best in Victoria. And let's not forget their sweet and eclectic space, with thrift store flower vases, hand-crafted pottery plates and random little plastic animals. Whatever it is, they've got me hooked.

Grant is one of those magical chefs whose food is not easy to duplicate, due to its originality and uniqueness. His food follows the seasons, infused and garnished with fresh, foraged, earthy things. Layered flavours, colours and textures result in the most beautifully plated food, creating the cravings that keep us coming back over and over again. And while Part + Parcel is more lunchy than brunchy, I can guarantee that they will feed you something you'll love, and you will forget about all these silly rules—just as I did.

PART + PARCEL

2656
QUADRA STREET

→ partandparcel.ca →

778.406.0888

Wheat Berry and Lentil Stew with Grilled Chicken Sausage and Duck Egg

> Oh, dear readers. For those of you who would like to cook like Grant Gard, I have shared his recipe here with you as he did with me. I have also provided some home-cook options to make it a wee bit easier on you.

TO MAKE THE MUSHROOM POWDER

In a dehydrator, dehydrate the mushroom slices for 36 hours at 150°F.

Place them in a spice grinder, and pulse until you have a fine powder. Use a pastry brush to sweep them into a new storage container. Keep them covered in a cool, dry place until ready to use or for up to 3 weeks.

TO MAKE THE CHARRED ONION DUCK STOCK

In a large pan, heat the oil over high heat. Add the onions, cut side down, and turn down the heat to medium-high. Don't move the onions, but let them cook for 5–7 minutes, until charred and dark. Remove and discard the onions. Add the wine and scrape the bottom of the pan with a wooden spoon to incorporate all of the brown bits. Bring the wine to a soft boil, then turn down to a simmer for 15–20 minutes and allow the wine to reduce by half. Add the water, duck legs, carrots, celery, salt, peppercorns, star anise and parsley. Bring to a boil over medium-high heat, then turn down to a simmer. Cook over low heat, covered, for about 90 minutes, until the duck is tender.

Remove the duck legs from the pan, shred the meat from the bone with a fork and freeze it for later use. Strain the liquid through a fine mesh sieve and set aside.

TO MAKE THE CHICKEN SAUSAGE

Using your hands, combine the chicken, chicken skin, shallot, garlic, parsley and salt in a medium bowl. Transfer to a large plate and place in the freezer for 15 minutes. Remove from the freezer and put it through a meat grinder, set to small die. Alternatively, pulse in a food processor until it takes on a ground texture. Do not over-process, as the meat will become gummy.

Put the meat mixture back in the freezer for 10 minutes and then into the bowl of a stand mixer fitted with the paddle attachment.

In a small bowl, whisk the egg, whipping cream and flour together. With the mixer running on low speed, slowly add this to the meat. Once all of the cream mixture has been added, increase the speed to medium and mix for 2–4 minutes, until the mixture looks sticky. Place the bowl in the refrigerator for 15 minutes.

Mushroom Powder

6 large cremini mushrooms, thinly sliced

Home cook option: Purchase a 2-oz bag of dried mushrooms (any kind you like) and grind them in a spice grinder, or use a mortar and pestle to grind them by hand.

Charred Onion Duck Stock

¼ cup neutral cooking oil

2 yellow onions, peeled and halved

1 cup dry red wine

5 cups water

4 duck legs

2 carrots, peeled and cut into ½-inch dice

2 stalks celery, cut into ½-inch dice

1½ tsp kosher salt

10 black peppercorns

1 star anise

1 bunch of flat-leaf parsley

Home cook option: Purchase 6 cups of good quality duck stock or chicken stock from your butcher.

Chicken Sausage

1 lb skinned and deboned chicken thighs, diced

¼ lb chicken skin, diced

1 medium shallot, peeled and roughly chopped

1 garlic clove, peeled and roughly cut

3 Tbsp chopped flat-leaf parsley

2½ tsp kosher salt

1 egg

⅓ cup whipping (35%) cream

1 Tbsp all-purpose flour

Lay two 24-inch-long pieces of plastic wrap on top of each other on a clean work surface. Place half of the sausage mixture on top and roll it into a tight log. Wrap the double layer of plastic tightly around the sausage log. Tie both ends very tightly, making sure there are no air pockets. Repeat with two more pieces of plastic wrap and the remaining meat mixture. In a sous vide machine, poach at 150°F for 2 hours.

Transfer to an ice bath to chill for about 5 minutes. Remove the plastic wrap and slice the sausages into the desired thickness. Set aside. Sausages can be wrapped and refrigerated for a day or two, or until ready to use.

HOME COOK OPTION

Place a large pot of water over medium-low heat and find a bowl that just fits inside the pot, upside down, leaving plenty of room for the water above (this prevents the wrapped sausage from touching the bottom of the pan and sticking). Bring the water up to 150°F. Maintaining this temperature for 2 hours is the trickiest part; however, this is a good solution if you don't have a sous vide machine! Add the wrapped sausage to the water, on top of the upside-down bowl, but still under water, and allow to cook, uncovered, for 2 hours. If the water gets too low, keep another pot on the stove at low heat and add to the big pot if needed.

TO MAKE THE WHEAT BERRIES

Heat 2 cups of water in a medium pot over low heat until it just starts to simmer slightly. Add the wheat berries. Keeping the water at a low simmer without boiling and, stirring often, heat the wheat berries for about 20 minutes, until plump and tender. Remove from the heat, cool in the cooking liquid, drain and set aside.

TO MAKE THE LENTILS

Heat 2 cups of water in a medium pot over low heat until it just starts to simmer slightly. Add the lentils. Keeping the water at a low simmer without boiling and stirring often, heat the lentils for about 20 minutes, until plump and tender. Remove from the heat, cool in the cooking liquid, drain and set aside.

TO MAKE THE RUTABAGA

Add the butter to a frying pan over low heat to melt. Add the diced rutabaga and cook, stirring often, for about 15 minutes, until the pieces start to soften and are lightly browned. Add salt to taste and cook for another 7–10 minutes, until soft but not mushy. Remove from the heat and set aside.

Home cook option: Purchase 1 lb of your favourite chicken sausages from your butcher.

Wheat Berries
½ cup wheat berries, rinsed

Lentils
½ cup lentils du Puy, sorted for stones and rinsed

Rutabaga
2½ Tbsp unsalted butter
1 rutabaga, peeled and cut into ½-inch dice
Salt

To make the stew
1 Tbsp extra virgin olive oil
1 yellow onion, finely diced
½ cup kale, tough stems removed, rinsed and chopped

To assemble
4 duck eggs (or chicken eggs)
1 Tbsp butter
Kosher salt and ground black pepper
Extra virgin olive oil
Sherry vinegar
Maldon salt
Chickweed, miner's lettuce, baby mustard greens, chives or other greens, for garnish

TO MAKE THE STEW

In a large pot over medium-high heat, warm the olive oil until shimmering. Add the onions and cook for 5–7 minutes, until softened. Add the duck broth, lentils, wheat berries and mushroom powder. Bring to a gentle simmer and then turn the heat down to as low as it will go to keep the stew warm until ready to serve. Just before serving, add the kale and simmer until wilted, about 5 minutes.

TO ASSEMBLE

Grill the chicken sausage. (If you are using links from your butcher, cut links into thirds.) Cover with foil to keep warm.

Fry the eggs. (See page 185.)

Add the butter to the stew and stir to combine. Season with kosher salt and ground black pepper to taste and about 2 Tbsp of olive oil. Ladle the stew into four warm bowls.

Place an egg on top of each bowl of stew. Arrange a few pieces of rutabaga on the stew around the egg. Finish with a drizzle of olive oil, a splash of sherry vinegar, Maldon salt, pepper and green garnish of your choice.

PICNIC

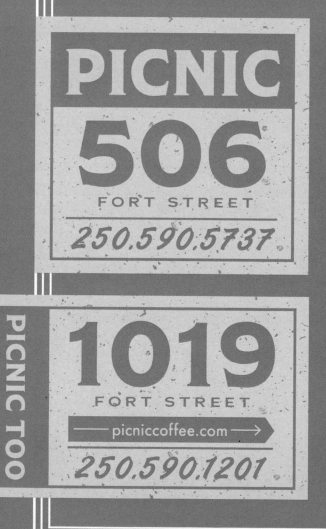

PICNIC
506
FORT STREET
250.590.5737

PICNIC TOO
1019
FORT STREET
picniccoffee.com →
250.590.1201

If you take a look at PicNic's social media pages, you will see a fantastic array of unique and delicious breakfast and brunch dishes on display. While this stylish space may pass as a simple coffee shop, be sure to stop in for some creative and thoughtful breakfast and lunch dishes from their ever-changing menu. PicNic and PicNic Too, their second location, both tiny spots on lower and upper Fort St., are in perfect locations to stay and enjoy all they have to offer or to grab and go before heading down to the Inner Harbour for brunch by the water. Great music, local 2% Jazz coffee and an array of delicious house-made food and drinks make PicNic the perfect stop.

Creamy Polenta with Roasted Veg and Chorizo

This is a warm and comforting dish that is a great fit for breakfast with the family on a lazy long weekend. Whip this up any time of year, roasting the veg and browning the chorizo the day before to minimize time spent in the cold kitchen the morning of.

Roasted Mushrooms, Tomatoes and Chorizo

1 lb your favourite mushrooms, washed and quartered
1 pint of cherry tomatoes, sliced in half
¼ cup extra virgin olive oil
1 Tbsp balsamic vinegar
Pinch of sea salt
Pinch of coarsely ground black pepper
3 links good-quality chorizo

Polenta

4 cups water
1 tsp sea salt
3 Tbsp unsalted butter
1 cup cornmeal
½ cup freshly grated Parmesan
1 tsp fresh thyme leaves

To assemble

8 large eggs
¼ cup chopped fresh basil leaves
Salt and ground black pepper

TO MAKE THE ROASTED MUSHROOMS, TOMATOES AND CHORIZO

Preheat the oven to 375°F.

Toss the mushrooms and tomatoes together in a large bowl. Add the oil, vinegar, salt and pepper and toss to blend well. Spread the mixture on a baking tray and bake for 20–25 minutes, until the vegetables are softened and slightly browned, giving it a stir about halfway through. Leave the tray on the stovetop, covered in aluminum foil, to keep warm.

Remove the casings from the chorizo and fry in a large frying pan over medium-high heat for about 10 minutes, until the meat is cooked through and slightly crispy.

TO MAKE THE POLENTA

Place the water and salt in a large pan over high heat. Bring to a boil. Turn down the heat to medium-low, add the butter and stir to melt it. Once the butter has melted, slowly add the cornmeal while whisking quickly to avoid lumps. Add the Parmesan and thyme. Keep stirring for 4–5 minutes, until the polenta is soft and creamy. Remove from the heat and cover to keep warm.

TO ASSEMBLE

Poach the eggs. (See page 183.)

Divide the warm polenta between four serving bowls. Top with the mushroom-tomato mixture, chorizo and two eggs each. Top with basil, season with salt and pepper and serve warm.

Q AT THE EMPRESS

I can't really write about Victoria without mentioning the Empress, can I? The grand hotel has gone through several changes over the past few years, one of the most extreme, perhaps, being the new restaurant, Q at the Empress. Introducing a bright, new expression of modern, Q is nothing if not classy, maintaining the Empress's highest standards for local food and drink.

Q represents a tribute to Queen Victoria, of course, and here you'll find the coolest series of art pieces—one set depicting the queen as a young woman, created in a modernized sort of old-fashioned colour-washed style, the other set showing her in her later years, with a bright, splashy art nouveau spirit to it. This dichotomy represents the space as a whole. Old meets new. Modern meets classic. Heritage meets present-day. A modern twist on royalty, indeed; it continues to hold a spiritedness within the aged walls.

The restaurant itself offers many options, so choosing a recipe for this book (yes, after trying them all) was not easy! Stick to simplicity, I say, then add a splash of complexity with a savoury brunch cocktail or two.

Q AT THE EMPRESS

721
GOVERNMENT STREET
→ qattheempress.com →
250.389.2727

Shrimp and Brie Omelette

SERVES 2

A simple yet elegant recipe that uses local ingredients (try side-striped shrimp from Finest at Sea [page 252] and Comox brie), this little omelette is a perfect Sunday morning treat! Serve it with roasted potatoes and hot coffee, and if you have some edible flowers in your garden, they make a lovely garnish.

½ tsp extra virgin olive oil
3 cups fresh stemmed and washed spinach
1 cup vegetable stock
1 Tbsp fresh lemon juice
1 Tbsp dry white wine (or additional lemon juice)
1 tsp chili flakes
6 oz raw side-striped shrimp
6 large eggs
1 Tbsp unsalted butter, divided
4 oz brie, thinly sliced
1 small tomato, cut into 4 wedges
Extra virgin olive oil, for drizzling
Salt and ground black pepper

Heat the olive oil in a medium frying pan over medium heat and swirl to cover the bottom. Add the spinach and stir for about 3 minutes, until wilted. Remove from the heat, let cool, roughly chop and season with salt and pepper.

In a medium pot over high heat, bring the vegetable stock, lemon juice, white wine and chili flakes to a boil. Add the shrimp, and poach for 30 seconds to 1 minute, until the shrimp are firm. Remove them from the pan with a slotted spoon and spread them out on a plate. Let cool enough to handle, then peel them and remove the tails.

In a medium bowl, beat the eggs and season to taste with salt and pepper.

In a small to medium non-stick or cast iron pan, melt ½ Tbsp of the butter. Add half the beaten eggs and allow them to spread over the surface of the pan. Let them cook for a few minutes, or until the eggs just begin to set. Using a silicone spatula, push the cooked parts of the omelette into the uncooked centre and allow to set again. Continue until the eggs are mostly set. They should still be soft and not too dry.

Place half the cheese, half the spinach and half the shrimp on one half of the omelette, flip the other side over to cover them and, using a spatula, lift the omelette onto a plate for serving. Repeat with the remaining ½ Tbsp of butter, eggs, cheese, spinach and shrimp. Serve immediately alongside the tomato wedges, drizzle with olive oil, and season with salt and pepper.

Empress Vodka Caesar

MAKES
4–6
COCKTAILS

Mixing the ingredients at least a day before allows the components to mingle and infuse and makes for a delicious blend. Don't add the vodka until you're ready to serve, as each cocktail will be built individually. The Caesar shown here is served with a charcoal-spiced rim, available exclusively at Q at the Empress, though the celery-salted rim is just as nice.

4 cups Motts Clamato juice
2 oz fresh lime juice
1½ oz Worcestershire sauce
½ oz balsamic vinegar
1 Tbsp Tabasco sauce
1 fresh garlic clove, minced
1 Tbsp fresh grated horseradish
1 tsp finely minced white onion
1 tsp ground black pepper
½ tsp kosher salt
½ tsp celery seeds
2 Tbsp fine salt
2 Tbsp celery salt
8–12 oz vodka
4–6 stalks pickled asparagus
4–6 green olives with pimento
4–6 lime wheels

In a large container, mix the Clamato juice, lime juice, Worcestershire, vinegar, Tabasco, garlic, horseradish, onion, pepper, kosher salt and celery seeds. Refrigerate for at least 4 hours, or up to overnight.

When ready to serve, mix together the 2 Tbsp fine salt and 2 Tbsp celery salt in a shallow bowl. Swipe the rims of tall glasses with a lime and twist in the salt mixture. Add 2 oz of your favourite vodka to each glass and fill to the top with ice cubes. Add the Clamato mix to fill the glass. Garnish with asparagus, olives and lime wheels.

RELISH FOOD AND COFFEE

Jamie Cummins opened Relish before many of the other small, casual and high-quality counter service restaurants started popping up in Victoria. We are a relaxed folk with high food standards here on the West Coast, and Relish's dishes reflect that perfectly. The menu changes regularly, but it is always full of local, organic and housemade items, such as bread, bacon, sausage and preserves. Relish has a fiercely loyal following (lovers of the Crispy Smoked Chicken are particularly loyal) and offers an array of dishes that are diverse and eclectic. Relish has always held a special place in my heart, and as an enthusiastic home chef, I am often inspired by Jamie's food. I look forward to seeing what he comes up with next.

RELISH
FOOD AND COFFEE

920
PANDORA AVENUE
— relishfoodcoffee.com →
250.590.8464

Rockfish Congee

SERVES
4-6

Congee is a type of rice porridge, popular in many Asian countries. Jasmine rice is a good choice for congee, though any long- or short-grain white rice will do. Rockfish, also known as rock cod or Pacific snapper, has a sweet, mild flavour that goes well with the spicy ingredients in the congee, and the kombu, an edible kelp, gives us a hit of iron and iodine and a whole host of minerals that benefit our health.

TO MAKE THE FRIED ROCKFISH

Thinly slice the cod into long pieces. In a bowl, combine the sambal oelek and sesame oil. Add the fish to the bowl, cover and allow to marinate in the refrigerator for at least 30 minutes, up to overnight. Remove the fish from the marinade, shaking off any excess marinade, and season with the salt. Pour the potato starch into a shallow bowl and dredge the fish through it, shaking off excess starch as you go. In a large frying pan, heat 2 Tbsp of oil over high heat. Fry the fish for 2–3 minutes per side, until golden.

TO MAKE THE CONGEE

Make this while the fish is marinating. In a large pot over high heat, bring the water to a boil. Remove from the heat and add the shiitakes. Cover the pot with a lid and allow the shiitakes to steep for 20 minutes. Remove from the water and set aside. Add the kombu to the water to steep for 40 minutes. Remove and discard (or eat!) the kombu. Add the chicken stock and the salt. Bring to a simmer over medium heat. Stir in the cooked rice, keeping the liquid at a simmer and stirring frequently. Continue to simmer for 15–20 minutes, until the mixture has the consistency of porridge. While the congee cooks, finely slice the shiitake mushrooms and then set them aside. Add the minced ginger to the congee and remove the pot from the heat. Add the fish sauce, then set aside, covering it to keep warm.

TO ASSEMBLE

In a small frying pan, melt the butter over medium heat. Pan-fry the corn until soft and lightly browned. Set aside and cover to keep warm.

Soft-poach the eggs. (See page 183.)

Ladle hot congee into four to six serving bowls. Top each one with a poached egg, corn, shiitakes, cilantro, scallions, sesame seeds, hot sauce of your choice and salt and pepper to taste.

Fried Rockfish

20 oz rock cod fillets, skin on
1 Tbsp sambal oelek
3 tsp sesame oil
2 tsp salt
4 Tbsp potato starch
Olive oil, for frying

Congee

8 cups water
12 pieces dried shiitake mushroom
2 pieces kombu
2 cups chicken stock
2 tsp kosher salt
4 cups cooked jasmine rice
    (about 2 cups uncooked)
1 generous Tbsp finely minced
    ginger (about 1½ inches)
1½ Tbsp fish sauce

To assemble

1 Tbsp unsalted butter
½ cup fresh or frozen corn
4–6 large eggs
1 bunch of cilantro, washed
8 scallions, chopped
Sesame seeds
Chili oil, garlic chili sauce or more
    sambal oelek, for serving
Salt and ground black pepper

THE RUBY

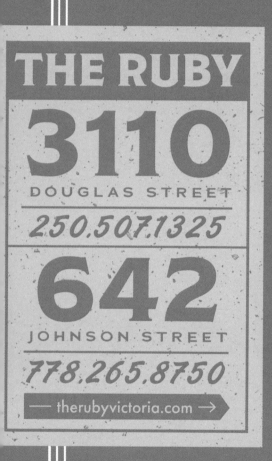

THE RUBY

3110
DOUGLAS STREET
250.507.1325

642
JOHNSON STREET
778.265.8750

— therubyvictoria.com →

Stepping into The Ruby on Johnson St. is like stepping back in time—with a twist. With antique taxidermy mounted above wallpaper adorned with roosters and chickens and a fantastic collection of classic vinyl, the space exudes an awesome mix of vintage and contemporary. Quirky and cool, this is reflected in the food, too. Old classics such as waffles and bennies and omelettes (oh, my) are elevated with duck confit, signature rubbed rotisserie chicken and, of special note, beef brisket inspired by the recipes from Ruby's brother restaurant, Jones Bar-B-Que on Cook St. The Ruby on Douglas St. is housed in the bright, eclectic Z Hotel, with the same high quality of food made by The Ruby's talented and creative chefs. Both Rubys serve breakfast until 3:00 pm, so if you are one of those people who prefer a late start, you won't miss out. Tuck yourself into a window table and order up anything from a quinoa porridge to a variety of breakfast tacos.

If you are a live music fan, particularly of Vancouver Island's famous Rock the Shores, you may be familiar with the folks from The Ruby. Their catering company, Alibi Catering, provides food to both performers and guests, and they offer the same stellar food and personalized restaurant-style experience at big and small events around town.

The Ruby's Skinny Hash

A healthier alternative to hollandaise and bacon without missing out on taste, this shredded potato and yam hash is a perfect weekday brunch. Reduce the balsamic and cook the vegetables in advance, and this dish comes together quickly.

1 cup balsamic vinegar
1 medium yam, skin on, scrubbed
4 Kennebec potatoes, skin on, scrubbed
Kosher salt and ground black pepper
9 eggs
Olive oil, for frying
1 large yellow onion, julienned
1½ cups sliced mushrooms of your choice
1–2 bunches of kale (about 8 cups, loosely packed), tough stems removed and leaves chopped
½ cup shaved Parmesan cheese
Olive oil, for drizzling

Bring the balsamic to a boil in a small pot over high heat. Turn down the heat to a simmer and allow it to reduce for 15–20 minutes, until it coats the back of a spoon. You should end up with about ⅓ cup. Set aside.

Preheat the oven to 250°F.

Shred the yam and potatoes into a large bowl. Whisk 1 egg and add it to the potatoes, along with a dash of salt and pepper. Mix all the ingredients by hand, making sure the egg is well incorporated.

Heat a large frying pan over medium heat and add 1 Tbsp olive oil.

Shape the potato mixture into four large cakes about 1½ inches thick, and fry for 5–7 minutes per side, until both sides are golden brown. Fry in batches if necessary. Place them on a sheet pan and keep warm in the oven.

Wipe out the frying pan and add another 2 Tbsp olive oil. Add the onions, and cook over medium heat for 5–7 minutes, until translucent. Add the mushrooms and cook for about 8 minutes, until soft. Add the kale, a splash of water and a pinch of salt and pepper. Cover and steam for 3–5 minutes, until the kale is soft and chewable. Remove from the heat and cover to keep warm.

Poach the remaining eight eggs. (See page 183.)

Place one potato cake on each of four warm serving plates. Top with kale mixture and drizzle with balsamic reduction. Place two poached eggs on top of each and garnish with Parmesan cheese and a drizzle of olive oil. Season with salt and pepper and serve.

SPINNAKERS GASTRO BREWPUB

I would say that Spinnakers is the epitome of a good old pub. Having been around since 1984, and housed in a building built in 1884, it comes complete with all you could expect: beautifully crafted woodwork throughout, multiple outdoor patios boasting waterfront views, little offshoot intimate rooms and big, fun, bright spaces with a great variety of décor and detail. Not only do they serve great beer, they make it themselves—their brewery is right on the premises, pumping out an impressive selection. Of course, all great pubs have top-of-the-line food, so let me introduce you to their stellar chef, Ali Ryan, whose amazing recipe compelled me to put her French toast on the front of this book! If you are visiting, be sure to inquire about Spinnaker's charming guest houses and check out the Provisions Store at the entrance to the pub—it sells fresh baking, beer, malt vinegar, a selection of house-made items and a ton more. Lucky for us, Spinnakers in Vic West is not the only place to enjoy their bounty of offerings. Spinnakers Spirit Merchant carries a variety of brews, spirits and wine, and Spinnakers on the Fly, in Victoria International Airport, allows us one last taste before leaving the island. I love Spinnaker's tagline: Let Nobody Thirst. They are most certainly doing a great job of that.

SPINNAKERS GASTRO BREWPUB

308 CATHERINE STREET

spinnakers.com

250.386.2739

Dark Ale Caramel Toast with Espresso Whip

Spinnakers' own Cascadia Dark Ale, the Red Fife sourdough and their house-made granola are available in the Provisions Store at the pub; local Fernwood coffee is used for the espresso whip.

TO MAKE THE CARAMEL TOAST

In a medium-sized pan over medium heat, simmer the dark ale for 10–15 minutes, until reduced by half. Set one half of the reduction aside for the Beer Caramel (see below). Cut the sourdough into 1-inch-thick slices and set aside.

In a medium-sized pan over medium heat, bring the brown sugar, butter and corn syrup to a light boil, stirring constantly. Remove immediately from the heat and mix in one half of the reduced beer to make a syrup.

Divide the beer syrup between two 9 × 13-inch lasagna pans. It should coat the bottom of the pans. Lay the bread in the syrup. Do not overlap. Combine the granulated sugar and ¼ tsp of the cinnamon and sprinkle it over the bread.

In a medium bowl, whisk together the eggs, milk, vanilla, salt and the remaining ¼ tsp of cinnamon. Pour this evenly over the bread in both pans. Cover with plastic wrap and refrigerate for at least 2 hours, or up to overnight.

Preheat the oven to 350°F.

Bake the pans of bread, uncovered, for about 20 minutes. When the egg mixture looks cooked and the bread is hot, carefully flip the bread over and sprinkle 1 Tbsp of granola over each pan.

TO MAKE THE BEER CARAMEL

Place the remaining half of the reduced beer, the brown sugar, butter and salt in a large pot over high heat. Bring the mixture to a boil, then turn down the heat to low and simmer gently for about 5 minutes, stirring with a silicone spatula only if it's about to boil over. Remove from the heat and stir in the cream. Cover and set aside.

TO MAKE THE ESPRESSO WHIPPING CREAM

In a stand mixer fitted with the whip attachment, or in a bowl and using an electric hand mixer, whip the cream and cold espresso on high speed until the cream is firm and has soft peaks.

TO ASSEMBLE

Plate two to three pieces of toast per guest. Drizzle with the caramel and dollop whipping cream on top. Sprinkle the remaining 2 Tbsp of granola overtop.

Caramel Toast

1 (650 ml) bottle dark ale
1 loaf of day-old Red Fife sourdough (or any sourdough)
2 cups brown sugar, packed
½ cup unsalted butter
2½ Tbsp dark corn syrup
¼ cup granulated sugar
½ tsp ground cinnamon, divided
6 large eggs
⅔ cup whole milk
1 tsp pure vanilla extract
1 pinch of sea salt
4 Tbsp granola, divided

Beer Caramel

2 cups brown sugar, packed
½ cup unsalted butter
½ tsp sea salt
½ cup whipping (35%) cream

Espresso Whipping Cream

2 cups whipping (35%) cream
1 shot (1 oz) espresso, chilled

Caramel expands when cooking, so be sure to start with a large pot. It's important to keep your eye on it, as it gets extremely hot very quickly!

THE SUMMIT RESTAURANT
AT THE VILLA EYRIE RESORT

By the time you've waited in line at any one of our many brunch places in Victoria, you could already be at The Summit and tucking into your first pancake! Aptly named for its location at the top of Malahat Dr. on Highway 1, The Summit boasts the most breathtaking views of the Saanich Inlet and has award-winning chefs in its state-of-the-art kitchen and a menu full of locally sourced, seasonal and Italian-inspired cuisine. And while you're at The Villa, be sure to include a little self-care by treating yourself to a visit to the Tuscan Spa. With the same gorgeous view of the inlet, the spa offers treatments that use local herbs and, wherever possible, the finest organic ingredients. Be sure to include a glass of wine with your treatment while you enjoy your little getaway just outside of town.

THE SUMMIT RESTAURANT

600
EBADORA LN., MALAHAT BC

villaeyrie.com →

250.856.0188

Pumpkin Pancakes

This recipe puts me in mind of cool, sunny autumn mornings, but using canned pumpkin purée makes these pancakes easy to whip up any time of year. Orange marmalade goes well with the spicy pumpkin flavour, though an apple compote or a citrusy whipped cream will also work.

1 cup unsalted butter,
   at room temperature
¼ cup finely chopped roasted
   chestnuts (or any other
   roasted nut)
1 tsp finely chopped orange zest
2 cups buttermilk
⅓ cup pumpkin purée
   (not pumpkin pie filling)
3 Tbsp unsalted butter, melted
1 tsp pure vanilla extract
1 large egg
1¼ cups all-purpose flour
¼ cup granulated sugar
1½ tsp baking powder
½ tsp baking soda
1 tsp grated lemon zest
¼ tsp pumpkin spice blend
   (or combine equal amounts of
   ground cinnamon, ginger, nutmeg,
   allspice, cloves)
Vegetable oil, for frying
Maple syrup, for serving
Orange marmalade, for serving
Icing sugar, for serving

Place the 1 cup butter, nuts and orange zest in a food processor fitted with the steel blade and mix well, until the ingredients are incorporated and the butter is fluffy. Scrape it onto a large piece of waxed paper and roll it into a log, about 1 inch in diameter. Twist the ends of the waxed paper tightly and refrigerate for at least 2 hours, or until ready to use. Extra butter can be kept wrapped tightly in the refrigerator for a week or in the freezer for up to 2 months.

Preheat the oven to 200°F.

In a large bowl, whisk together the buttermilk, pumpkin purée, melted butter, vanilla and egg. In a medium bowl, whisk together the flour, sugar, baking powder, baking soda, lemon zest and pumpkin spice. Add the dry ingredients to the wet ingredients in four additions, folding in each addition before adding the next batch. Do not overmix. It's okay if the mixture is a bit lumpy.

Heat about 1 Tbsp of vegetable oil in a large cast iron pan over medium heat. Pour about ¼ cup of batter into the centre of the pan, spreading it out with a ladle to about 4 inches in diameter. Once bubbles start to form at the edges of the pancake, after about 2 minutes, flip the pancake and cook for another 2 minutes, until nicely browned and cooked through. Keep warm in the oven until all the pancakes are cooked.

Remove the nut butter from the fridge and slice it into ¼-inch discs. Plate the pancakes, top with butter, maple syrup and orange marmalade, and sprinkle with icing sugar. Serve hot.

TONOLLI'S DELI

Tonolli's Deli is a quaint little place in Central Saanich, run by two ambitious Hungarian sisters who had a vision to bring authentic European flavours to Victoria. The beautiful bread and other baking is made fresh every morning, and the menu offers a fantastic selection of dishes, complete with all-day breakfasts and lunches. The dining room is adorned with floral curtains and seat cushions and a charm that makes this place a perfect spot for a lingering brunch or a quick bite. Stop in on Pizza Fridays to pick up a slice of a pie and grab a pastry or two to top it off. Slightly off the beaten path, this is a little hidden treasure that definitely deserves a visit.

TONOLLI'S DELI

6991
EAST SAANICH ROAD
tonollisdeli.com →
778.426.2822

French Baked Eggs with White Truffle Cream

This is a delicious and decadent dish great for the weekend or a special occasion. The white truffle cream is imported from Italy and available for purchase at Tonolli's, but if you can't find it, replace it with an extra 1 Tbsp of cream plus 2 tsp of white truffle oil. (Or try Charelli's [page 214]—they often carry it.) Serve these with toasted French baguette to scoop it all up.

12 oz thinly sliced cotto ham
4 oz brie, sliced into 4
8 large eggs
½ cup shredded white cheese
   (mozzarella, Edam, white cheddar
   are all good options)
½ cup table (18%) cream
2 tsp white truffle cream
2 Tbsp finely chopped curly parsley

Preheat the oven to 400°F.

Line four 10-inch ramekins on the bottom and up the sides with the thinly sliced ham. Place a slice of brie in the centre of the ham slices. Crack two eggs and place one on either side of the brie in each ramekin. Sprinkle the shredded cheese over the eggs, carefully covering each yolk completely.

Whisk the cream and truffle cream together and pour it gently over the eggs and cheese in each ramekin. Place the ramekins on a baking tray and pour about ¼ inch of water around the ramekins. Bake for 12–15 minutes. The eggs are cooked soft to medium when the cheese is bubbling and lightly browned on top. Add about 5 more minutes if you prefer a well-done egg. Remove from the oven, let sit for 5 minutes and sprinkle with parsley before serving.

THE VILLAGE RESTAURANT

THE VILLAGE RESTAURANT

2518 ESTEVAN AVENUE
250.592.8311

4517 W. SAANICH ROAD
778.265.8898

4087 SHELBOURNE STREET
778.265.5200

— thevillagerestaurant.ca →

As a supplement to the food coming from some of our best local island farms and food suppliers, The Village sources a portion of their produce, literally, from their own backyards. Co-owners Jason and Brian have taken the task of sourcing food into their own hands by growing all kinds of fresh veggies including kale, salad greens, and herbs in their own backyards, and right on the patios at each of the three locations. This process of supplying The Village has come to be known affectionately as the #VILLAGEgrowshow, and it is The Village's intention to expand on this small-scale, organic and satisfying way of growing and supplying their restaurants. You really can't get any fresher than that.

The Village's spaces are fun and bright, and the food and drinks are thoughtful and enticing. I am a big fan of these guys and their quest to make wonderful food for all of us, while contributing to community, the environment and a warm and welcoming neighbourhood feel.

Red Shakshouka

SERVES
4

This is a versatile dish that blends the fresh taste of tomatoes with the creaminess of poached eggs. Serve this over roasted potatoes; add sausage or bacon, grilled mushrooms or chickpeas; or simply dip toasted rye in the yolk and sauce for a simple and delicious breakfast.

TO MAKE THE SHAK SPICE

Mix all the ingredients together in an airtight container. This will keep in a cool, dark place for 3 months.

TO MAKE THE RED SHAKSHOUKA

Heat 1 Tbsp of the olive oil in a large, shallow frying pan over medium heat. Add the spinach, and toss with tongs until it's coated in the olive oil. Add the sliced garlic and toss so the garlic doesn't burn. Add a drop or two of water if the pan gets too dry to steam the spinach. Toss for 4–5 minutes, until the spinach is fully wilted and any liquid has cooked off. Remove from the heat and set aside.

In a large pot over medium-high heat, sauté the onions and minced garlic in the remaining olive oil for about 10 minutes, until soft but not brown.

Add the shak spice, tomatoes and salt. Bring to a boil, then turn down the heat to a simmer and cook for 45 minutes, stirring often to avoid burning.

TO ASSEMBLE

Poach the eggs. (See page 183.)

Divide the red shakshouka evenly between four shallow bowls. Top each bowl with spinach, two poached eggs and parsley, and lay rye toast on the side for dipping and scooping. Serve immediately.

Shak Spice
¼ cup paprika
¼ cup ground cumin
¼ cup ground turmeric
¼ cup curry powder

Red Shakshouka
2 Tbsp extra virgin olive oil, divided
1 bunch of spinach, washed, stemmed and chopped
1–2 garlic cloves, thinly sliced
1 white onion, julienned
3 garlic cloves, minced
2 Tbsp shak spice
2 (each 14 oz) cans diced tomatoes with juice
2 tsp kosher salt

To assemble
8 large eggs
2 Tbsp minced flat-leaf or curly parsley
8 slices rye bread, toasted and buttered

VIS À VIS
BOUCHON BAR

The name *Vis à Vis* refers to a "face-to-face" meeting between two people. The thought of this inspires me to call a friend for a catch-up visit and a glass of wine. Or to round up a few friends for an intimate gathering in a small, candle-lit room with good food and cocktails. Or simply to sidle up solo to the bar to enjoy a drink and a chat with the bartender to wrap up the week. If any of these scenarios inspire you too, this is the place to make them happen. I remember the first time I walked into Vis à Vis in Oak Bay Village. The incredible décor showcases exposed brick walls, beautiful retro hanging light pendants, hand-scripted chalkboards and exquisite ironwork details. The room is warm and inviting; perfect for getting a little bit lost in over a local brew or two with a meat and cheese board made with products from neighbouring shops, a bowl of West Coast mussels or the chef's fresh fish feature. Or maybe brunch will be your reason to visit, to hang out on the little street-side patio, watching the hustle and bustle as the people of Oak Bay pass on by.

VIS À VIS
BOUCHON BAR

2228
OAK BAY AVENUE
— visavisoakbay.com →
250.590.7424

Duck Confit Hash

SERVES 4

> If making your own duck confit doesn't suit you, try The Whole Beast Artisan Salumeria (page 278) for duck confit, already prepared.

TO MAKE THE DUCK CONFIT

Mix the raw duck legs, salt, sugar, bay leaf, thyme and lemon zest together in an airtight container and place in the refrigerator for 24 hours.

Preheat the oven to 300°F.

Place the duck fat in a casserole dish large enough to hold the fat and the duck legs and let it sit in the oven for about 10 minutes, until the duck fat is melted.

Remove the duck legs from their container, rinse and dry thoroughly with paper towel. Submerge the legs in the melted fat so they are completely covered. Cover tightly with aluminum foil and cook in the oven for about 2 hours. Remove the casserole dish from the oven, discard the foil, and let the legs cool in the fat. When ready to serve, remove the legs from the fat and shred the meat from the bones with a fork. Set aside.

TO MAKE THE HASH

Bring a large pot of water to boil over high heat. Add about 1 Tbsp salt. Add the potatoes and cook for 8–10 minutes, until just tender. Remove the pot from the heat, drain the potatoes and let cool.

Heat a large frying pan on medium heat. Add the duck fat to the pan and let it melt. Add the potatoes and fry in the duck fat until golden brown. Add the confit duck meat, scallions, chives, parsley and lemon juice. Season with salt and pepper and cover with aluminum foil to keep warm.

TO MAKE THE HOLLANDAISE

Whisk the egg yolks, white wine, salt and pepper together in a large metal bowl. Bring a large pot of water to a simmer on the stove over medium heat. Set the metal bowl inside the pot, ensuring the bottom of the bowl is not touching the water. Very slowly, drizzle in the clarified butter, whisking vigorously until the mixture is emulsified. Be sure not to overheat the mixture. Remove from the heat and gently stir in the lemon juice, Tabasco and Worcestershire sauce. Slowly fold in the grainy mustard and set aside.

TO ASSEMBLE

Poach the eggs. (See page 183.) Divide the hash between four warm shallow bowls. Top each with a poached egg, ¼ of the hollandaise sauce, and some arugula and scallions.

Duck Confit

8 raw duck legs
¼ cup kosher salt
¼ cup brown sugar, packed
4 bay leaves
20 sprigs of thyme
Zest of 4 lemons, roughly chopped
8 cups duck fat

Hash

4 lb fingerling potatoes, scrubbed
    and cut into ¼-inch coins
¼ cup duck fat
6 scallions, chopped
¼ cup chopped chives
¼ cup chopped flat-leaf parsley leaves
3 Tbsp fresh lemon juice
Kosher salt and ground black pepper

Hollandaise

3 large egg yolks
1 Tbsp dry white wine
1 tsp salt
1 tsp ground black pepper
1 cup clarified butter,
    (see page 189)
1 tsp lemon juice
1 tsp Tabasco sauce
1 tsp Worcestershire sauce
1 Tbsp grainy mustard

To assemble

4 large eggs
4 cups fresh arugula, dressed with
    a little olive oil, salt and pepper
2 scallions, finely chopped

Vis à Vis Once Upon a Swizzle

> If you get the chance, read Vis à Vis's entertaining and descriptive cocktail menu in-house or online. El Jimador Reposado tequila and Alvear Fino sherry are great for this drink.

TO MAKE THE GINGER SYRUP

If you have a juicer, peel the ginger and juice it to get ¼–⅓ cup of juice. If you don't have a juicer, place the ginger (with peel intact) in the freezer until solid. Remove from the freezer and let it thaw. Squeeze the juice out of the ginger by wringing it out with your hands and squeezing until all of the juice has been extracted.

Place the ginger juice in a blender, add the sugar and blend until the sugar is completely dissolved. The syrup will keep its fresh flavour in an airtight container in the refrigerator for about 2 weeks. Add 1 oz of vodka to the syrup to extend its storage life to 1 month.

TO ASSEMBLE

Combine the tequila, sherry, Liquore Strega, lime juice, grapefruit juice, a few shakes of ginger syrup, and bitters in a cocktail shaker. Add about 2 Tbsp of crushed ice and shake vigorously until the ice is dissolved. Fill two highball glasses with crushed ice and split the cocktail between the two. Stir and top with more crushed ice. Top with a few additional dashes of bitters and garnish with candied ginger and a mint sprig.

Ginger Syrup
12 oz fresh ginger
½ cup superfine sugar

To assemble
2 oz reposado tequila
1½ oz fino sherry
⅔ oz Liquore Strega
1½ oz fresh lime juice
1 oz fresh grapefruit juice
1½ Tbsp ginger syrup
Angostura bitters
Crushed ice
Candied ginger pieces, for garnish
Mint sprigs, for garnish

WILLIE'S CAFÉ AND BAKERY

Willie's Bakery dates back to 1887 and is a long-time Victoria institution. As you might have guessed, it is in a heritage building, at the bottom of lower Johnson St. (otherwise known as LoJo), next to Waddington Alley. The bakery was opened by a miller and baker named Louis Wille (as Wille's Bakery) and was run by four generations of Willes until 1976, when it closed. It was reopened by a different family in 1999 as Willie's Bakery.

Over the years, several renovations have been completed, maintaining the heritage of the building and the area, adding a beautiful brick garden patio on one side and refinishing the interior to match the original counter design. The history and the story of Willie's and that part of town, which is perfect to wander around and explore, is quite cool. You can learn more about Willie's history on their website.

Today, Willie's Bakery has an extensive menu of beautiful breakfast and lunch items, with a vast selection of bennies, baked goods, fresh soups, salads, sandwiches and burgers. Hang out on their sweet little garden patio in the summertime, or tuck in next to the fireplace indoors in the cooler months.

WILLIE'S CAFÉ AND BAKERY

537
JOHNSON STREET
willies.ca →
250.381.8414

Portobello Mushroom Benny

This benny is a bit different in that the hollandaise is made in a food processor and not cooked. It makes for a light, airy hollandaise with a bit of grainy Dijon and pesto to keep it grounded. The mushrooms add earthiness and umami, and the brioche, which you can get right at Willie's Bakery, is the perfect base.

Hollandaise

8 large egg yolks

¼ cup fresh lemon juice (2 lemons)

2 Tbsp hot sauce (such as Tabasco or Frank's Red Hot)

¾ cup clarified butter, cooled (see page 189)

1 Tbsp grainy Dijon mustard

1 Tbsp pesto sauce

2 pinches of kosher salt

To assemble

6 portobello mushrooms, washed, stems removed and gills scraped out with a teaspoon

2 Tbsp extra virgin olive oil

Sea salt and ground black pepper

6 cups baby spinach

12 large eggs

6 slices brioche, toasted and buttered

TO MAKE THE HOLLANDAISE

In the bowl of a food processor fitted with the steel blade, place the egg yolks, lemon juice and hot sauce. Blend for 1 minute. With the food processor running, add the clarified butter in a very slow drizzle until the sauce becomes thick and creamy.

Stop the machine, add the mustard, pesto and salt and blend for about 10 seconds to combine. If the hollandaise becomes too thick, add a little bit of hot water and blend again until it is a thick but pourable consistency.

Fill a pot with very tap hot water. Place a metal bowl over the water, making sure the bottom of the bowl is not touching the water. Scrape the hollandaise from the food processor into the metal bowl and set it aside to keep warm.

TO ASSEMBLE

Preheat the grill to about 350°F (medium-high heat). Brush the mushrooms all over with the olive oil and season to taste with salt and pepper. Grill for 5–7 minutes, then flip and grill for another 5 minutes, until the mushrooms have released some moisture and are nicely browned. Cut each mushroom in half and wrap in aluminum foil to keep warm.

Heat a large frying pan over medium heat. Add 1 Tbsp of water and all of the spinach. Using tongs, toss the spinach around for about 5 minutes, until wilted. Season with salt and pepper and cover the pan with a lid to keep warm.

Poach the eggs. (See page 183.)

Place a slice of brioche on each of six plates. Top with sautéed spinach, a portobello mushroom, two poached eggs and some hollandaise. Serve with a tossed green salad or roasted potatoes.

Willie's Bakery Carrot Cake

You would be missing out if we didn't include a bakery recipe from Willie's. I am so excited that they were willing to let me share this cake recipe with you. It is so delicious! The crunchy pecans on top give it that extra toasty flavour and the cream cheese icing has just the perfect amount of sweet.

Carrot Cake

3 cups all-purpose flour
1 Tbsp baking powder
1 Tbsp ground cinnamon
2½ tsp baking soda
1½ tsp sea salt
1½ tsp ground nutmeg
1 cup granulated sugar
1 cup brown sugar, packed
4 large eggs
1 cup vegetable oil
½ cup pineapple juice (you can use the juice from the can of pineapple)
1½ tsp pure vanilla extract
3 cups grated carrots
1½ cups unsweetened canned crushed pineapple
¾ cup chopped pecans

Cream Cheese Icing

3 (each ½ lb) packages plain full-fat cream cheese, softened
2 cups unsalted butter, softened
2 tsp pure vanilla extract
3 cups icing sugar
1 cup toasted, crushed pecans

TO MAKE THE CARROT CAKE

Preheat the oven to 325°F. Grease and flour the sides and bottom of two 9-inch round cake pans.

In a medium bowl, sift and whisk together the flour, baking powder, cinnamon, baking soda, salt and nutmeg. Set aside. In a large bowl, beat together both sugars, the eggs, oil, pineapple juice and vanilla until smooth.

Slowly pour the flour mixture into the egg mixture and stir until just evenly moistened. Stir in the carrots, pineapple and pecans. Divide this batter evenly between the two prepared pans and smooth the tops.

Bake in the centre of the oven for 1 hour, or until a cake tester or toothpick inserted in the centre comes out clean. Let the cakes cool in the pans on a wire rack.

TO MAKE THE CREAM CHEESE ICING

Meanwhile, using a handheld beater or a stand mixer fitted with the paddle attachment, beat together the cream cheese, butter, and vanilla for 3–4 minutes at high speed until blended. With the mixer running, slowly add the icing sugar and beat at high speed for 5–7 minutes, until light and fluffy.

TO ASSEMBLE

Place one cake on a cake stand and cover completely with icing as shown in the photo. Place the second cake on top and cover completely with icing as shown. Press the crushed pecans on top and enjoy.

ZAMBRI'S

Many of my memories of when I first moved to Victoria from Vancouver in 2004 revolve around the food scene at that time. It was around the early 2000s that Victoria's culinary offerings started to grow in giant leaps, with restaurants, cafés, coffee shops and markets opening every month.

The most popular spots, whether long-time pubs or new establishments who had gained a healthy following, weren't nearly as plentiful as they are today. Zambri's, however, which at the time was a small and welcoming space in the back end of a strip mall, was one of the few where you could expect to see a lineup on a regular basis. We found ourselves enticed by the authentic Italian soul food, the cozy, inviting room and the open kitchen. We watched pasta being flung, vegetables being roasted and grappa being poured. The gorgeous food and talented owners kept us coming back, and eventually, we all started to feel the squeeze in the intimate yet limited space. Luckily, the Zambris seized the moment to move to a bigger, brighter place, where they continue to dazzle the city. I have come to know the Zambri family a bit better over the years and continue to appreciate all they bring to us. Truly dedicated to their craft, they deserve all the accolades and admiration that come their way. *Salute!*

ZAMBRI'S

820
YATES STREET
zambris.ca →
250.360.1171

Zambri's Spaghetti e Aglio Olio Peperoncino with Fried Egg

SERVES 4

Bring on the breakfast pasta, I say. Marinated peperoncino is a beautiful addition to this dish and is great to have on hand in the fridge. Double the recipe and use it to top off anything and everything.

Zambri's Marinated Peperoncino

10 jalapeño peppers,
  sliced ¼-inch thick
3 garlic cloves, peeled
  but not chopped
Pinch of dried red chili flakes
Pinch of kosher salt
⅔ cup vegetable oil
⅓ cup extra virgin olive oil

Spaghetti

10 large garlic cloves, cut into
  about 4 or 5 slices per clove
1 jalapeño pepper, cut into rings
  about ¼-inch thick
⅓ cup extra virgin olive oil
3 Tbsp unsalted butter
Kosher salt and ground black pepper
Chili flakes (a pinch to a tsp
  depending on your preferred
  spice level)
3 Tbsp chopped flat-leaf parsley
14 oz dried spaghetti
4 large eggs
½ cup fine, dried breadcrumbs,
  plus more for serving
½ cup grated Parmigiano,
  plus more for serving
Ground black pepper

TO MAKE THE ZAMBRI'S MARINATED PEPERONCINO

Place the sliced jalapeños, garlic, dried chilies and salt in a medium pot over medium-high heat. Add enough of the vegetable and olive oil in a ratio of 2:1 to just cover the jalapeños. Bring the oils to a boil. Turn off the heat and let the ingredients steep until cooled. Place in a clean, airtight jar. This can be refrigerated for up to 2 weeks.

TO MAKE THE SPAGHETTI

Place eight slices of marinated peperoncino, the garlic, jalapeño, olive oil and butter in a large, cold frying pan and season with a pinch of salt and pepper. Turn on the heat to medium and cook, stirring, for about 5 minutes. Add the chili flakes and cook, stirring, for another 5–7 minutes, until the garlic is golden brown and the jalapeños look like they are softening. Add the parsley and cook for about 2 minutes, until the parsley is wilted and all the ingredients are well blended. Remove from the heat.

Preheat the oven to 170°F.

Place a large pot full of water over high heat. Add enough salt that the water tastes like seawater. Once the water is boiling, add the spaghetti and cook according to package directions.

Place four bowls in the warm oven. Drain the spaghetti, add it to the peperoncino mixture and toss until thoroughly coated with the oil and other ingredients. Season to taste with salt and pepper.

TO ASSEMBLE

Fry the eggs. (See page 185.)

Remove the bowls from the oven and sprinkle the bottom of each with some of the breadcrumbs and then some of the Parmigiano. Divide the spaghetti evenly between the bowls. Top with the remaining breadcrumbs and Parmigiano. Finish with a grind of black pepper.

THE
Almighty
EGG

"Put an egg on it." Follow this oft-used advice to transform any simple dish into a solid meal. But how you cook that egg, exactly, is up to you. And so, courtesy of the chefs and experts featured in this book, I bring you the ultimate guide to doing eggs right.

Poached Eggs

There is general agreement that using acidulated water to poach eggs is the best way. There is less agreement about the size of pot to use. A tall pot creates a poached egg that is more of a teardrop in shape, whereas a shallow pot will result in a flatter egg. Each of these shapes serves its own purpose. The teardrop shape lends itself to being tucked into a bed of roasted potatoes, for example, and the flatter version is ideal for sitting atop an English muffin. If you are super-fancy and want to avoid those wispy whites that sometimes trail from a poached egg, gently slide your raw egg into a fine mesh sieve before cooking. This drains off the more liquid-y white, and creates a rounder, smoother poached egg. And some say that you can skip the vinegar when using this method, as there are fewer wispy whites to coagulate.

Bring about 8 cups of water to a boil in a medium-sized pot over high heat. Crack a single egg into a small, shallow dish or ramekin. Turn down the heat to a gentle simmer and add 1 Tbsp of white vinegar to the pot. Stir the water to create a slight whirlpool in the centre (this helps the white wrap around the yolk) and slide the egg slowly and gently into the whirlpool. I have found that timings for poached eggs vary widely by stove. Whether you're using gas or electric, though, keep the water at a bare simmer. Typically, a medium poached egg, where the white is fully cooked and the yolk is creamy and runny, takes 3–4 minutes. Adjust with more or less time to get a soft- or a hard-poached egg. If you add more than one egg to the water, increase the time by 30–60 seconds. The more often you poach, the more accurate your timing will be.

Remove the egg from the water with a slotted spoon and tilt it onto a plate with a few layers of paper towel or a clean tea towel to absorb any excess liquid. Remember, if you are placing an egg onto hot food, it will continue to cook, so be sure to serve such a dish immediately.

Poaching for a Crowd

It's not always easy to poach a dozen eggs at a time. Especially when Uncle Bob prefers soft-poached and Cousin Betty prefers hard-poached. The answer is this: lightly pre-poach your eggs in batches, then return them to the simmering water when ready to serve. Note that if you are really pinched for time, you can poach eggs up to a day ahead, keeping them submerged in cold water in an airtight container in the refrigerator. Bring the eggs back to room temperature prior to re-poaching.

To pre-poach eggs, bring 8 cups of water to a boil in a large pot over high heat, then turn down the heat to a simmer. Add 1 Tbsp of vinegar to the water. Poach the eggs, two or three at a time, for 2–3 minutes. Remove the eggs from the water with a slotted spoon and gently submerge them in a bowl of ice cold water to stop the cooking, being very careful not to break them. Cover the bowl and set aside (or put it in the refrigerator) until ready to serve. Repeat this process until you have all the poached eggs you need. When it is time to plate your dishes, return the water on the stove to a very gentle simmer. Using a slotted spoon, carefully place one or two eggs at a time into the simmering water. For a soft-poached egg, simply leave the egg in the water for about 30 seconds, just to reheat it. For medium-poached, leave it in for 1–1½ minutes, and for hard-poached, 2–3 minutes should do it.

There are other options out there for poaching eggs in large numbers, such as the poaching pan, silicone poaching pods and the method where raw eggs are added to a muffin tin with a touch of water and baked in the oven. Personally, I prefer the natural shape an egg takes when poached in a pot of water, but research the others ways if you wish and use whatever method suits you best.

Boiled Eggs

Jen Woike from Farmer Ben's Eggs (see pages 248 and 292) passed on these failsafe tips for successfully boiling eggs. We all know the frustration that comes from anticipating a perfect hard-boiled egg, only to struggle with peeling it or finding a grey ring around the yolk. The trick? Don't boil your eggs. Steam them!

Put a pot on the stove with just enough water to stay below a steamer basket set inside. Load the basket with eggs—but don't go nuts. You want just a single layer in the bottom of the basket. Cover the pot and bring the water to a boil over medium-high heat. Turn down the heat to low and simmer, still covered, for 10 minutes (or about 6 minutes for soft or 8 minutes for medium-boiled eggs). It is difficult to ruin these eggs. Even overcooked they do not turn out rubbery or have that nasty grey ring. Turn off the heat and allow the eggs to sit, covered, for an additional 3–5 minutes and then cool them under cold running water or in an ice bath. Peel, and do a happy-dance over how impossibly easy that was!

I had never used this method before, so in test-kitchen fashion, I put it to the test. It worked beautifully! This is definitely my new boiled egg go-to.

Fried Eggs

oming from a food photographer's perspective, frying an egg for eating is relatively simple. Frying an egg for shooting is another story. For a perfect-looking egg that also tastes great, here are some tips.

Sunny-side-ups are the most challenging, because it's difficult to get the white cooked enough to be solid and the yolk cooked but still runny. Cooking an over-easy egg is a matter of doing just that—gently flipping the egg over and cooking for a short (easy) time. This ensures a soft yolk and a properly cooked white. Leave it longer and it becomes over-hard. You get the idea.

Method 1

Heat a small non-stick frying pan over medium-low heat. Add ½ tsp of butter and let it melt. Gently crack one egg into the pan, being careful not to break the yolk. Using a butter knife, immediately cut through the white of the egg just surrounding the yolk (without breaking the yolk itself). Starting at the edge of the yolk (without touching it) pull your knife outward towards the edge of the white to break it. This helps to cook the white evenly. Watch the egg carefully while it cooks. If it starts to form bubbles and the white starts to get dark on the edges, turn the heat down right away or lift the pan off the heat for a moment. Cook gently and slowly, until the white is set and the yolk is just cooked. This method will give you a crispy-edged egg, perfect for topping anything. Remove from the pan, season with salt and pepper and serve hot.

Method 2

This method has its advantages (less mess; perfectly cooked, stunning yolk) and disadvantages (not as crispy an edge, you have to turn the oven on) but it is one I use often, because the egg ends up perfectly picturesque and the whites cook evenly. Tiny, individual cast iron pans work best, but any ovenproof pan will do. Preheat the oven to 350°F. Add 1 tsp butter or oil to your pan and place it in the oven until the butter melts. Crack one egg into the pan and cook in the oven for about 8 minutes, until the white is just set. Remove from the pan with a silicone spatula, season with salt and pepper and serve hot (or immediately photograph and post to social media to show off your fried egg–cooking skills).

Scrambled Eggs

I prefer my scrambled eggs on the softer, creamier side. Some like them a bit drier and fully cooked. It's just a matter of how long you cook them. The trick to achieving delicious scrambled eggs is to always cook them low and slow, and the rule of thumb is that the eggs should never be browned. Many people add milk or cream to their eggs, but I have found that the water content in those ingredients make for wet, overcooked eggs. Whisk your eggs really well. Incorporating air will help with the fluffiness.

For perfectly scrambled eggs, melt 2 tsp butter in a frying pan over medium heat. In a medium bowl, vigorously whisk three large eggs. Once the butter has melted, pour the eggs into the pan. Let them sit for 30–60 seconds, just until you see the outer edges begin to set. Using a silicone spatula, move the eggs around, exposing the uncooked parts to the heat and moving the cooked parts into the centre. Lift the pan off the stove or turn the heat down if they are cooking too quickly. Keep the eggs moving, lifting and folding them, so they don't brown. They will be soft and quite lumpy. Once the eggs are just barely cooked (they will continue to cook for 30 seconds or so, once taken off the heat), remove them from the pan, season with salt and pepper and serve hot. This method results in soft and creamy scrambled eggs. If you are someone who prefers well-cooked scrambled eggs, simply increase the cooking time until the desired consistency is reached.

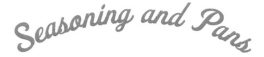

Seasoning and Pans

The almighty egg is one of the most underrated and overcooked ingredients in the kitchen. Whether you choose to fry it with a crispy edge or opt for a creamy scramble, the egg deserves some culinary respect! Some slow, gentle cooking, light seasoning, and the right pan will make all the difference.

Season eggs only once they are cooked. Adding salt too early can break down the eggs and make them watery. Also, in the case of a fried egg, salt will discolour the yolk and make it spotty, so if you're looking for visual perfection, offer salt at the table. And it likely goes without saying: freshly ground black pepper is best. But don't limit yourself to salt and pepper. Many other things can be added to season your eggs, either in the whisked eggs before cooking (fresh herbs, smoked paprika, cayenne, for example), or sprinkle cheese or your favourite spice or flavoured salt on top once the eggs are plated.

I prefer to use cast iron frying pans to cook eggs and will switch out the size, depending on how many eggs I'm cooking. It should be noted, though, that my cast iron pans are very well seasoned, and rarely is there an issue with sticking. The biggest challenge with cast iron is that it gets hot and stays hot, so lowering the heat when necessary isn't easy. (And you need to use an oven mitt when you touch the handle.) Definitely keep the temperature on the lower side when using cast iron. That being said, if you need to, embrace food-safe, non-stick pans! They are the perfect tools for cooking eggs that slide nicely onto the plate.

The Perfect Hollandaise

It's no secret that hollandaise can be tricky. As with mayonnaise or salad dressing, you want to emulsify its ingredients. Like oil and water, these ingredients aren't necessarily all that compatible. Here are a few tips and tricks for a thick and creamy hollandaise.

WHIP THE EGGS WELL WITH WATER AND ACID. Before setting the stainless steel bowl over the heat, use a wire whisk to whip the eggs well, lifting the whisk high and incorporating lots of air into the mixture.

MAKE SURE YOUR WATER ISN'T TOO HOT. High heat is the enemy of hollandaise, as instead of slowly cooking the eggs into a creamy sauce, it scrambles them. Instant fail. Use a thermometer to keep your water and your butter as close to 147°F as possible, until you get the hang of it.

MAKE YOUR BUTTER THE SAME TEMPERATURE AS YOUR EGG MIXTURE. Maintaining a consistent temperature helps to easily incorporate the butter into the eggs. If your butter is too hot, it may cook the eggs too quickly. If it is too cool, you may have trouble streaming it slowly into the egg mixture.

ADD YOUR BUTTER VERRRRY SLOWLY. This is a big one, and it is the secret to any successful emulsion. Trickle that butter in super slowly, in drops if you must, until it is fully incorporated. Also, don't add too much butter! You'll just end up with an oily mess.

EAT IT RIGHT AWAY. The butter and egg will start to separate if left for too long. Keeping the sauce in a heated thermos helps, but ideally, it's best consumed immediately.

Troubleshooting Hollandaise

A broken hollandaise can be disappointing. All is not lost, however, and though it won't be as smooth and creamy as it could have been, you can still make it completely acceptable. Whisk a room temperature yolk vigorously with about 1 Tbsp of tepid water in a large bowl. Slowly add the warm broken sauce, re-emulsifying it into the yolk. Continue to whisk until you have recreated a smooth sauce. Note that if you have accidentally overheated your hollandaise and scrambled the eggs, it is sadly beyond repair and your only option is to start again.

Jamie Cummins's Hollandaise Sauce

Everyone needs a good hollandaise sauce. There are many variations to add depth and flavour, but first you need to master the basics. Jamie Cummins from Relish Food and Coffee has generously shared with us his famous brunch holly. It really helps to have a kitchen thermometer, especially if this is your first time making it.

Add about 2 inches of water to a medium to large pot and bring to a simmer over medium heat. In a metal bowl that just fits inside the pot and doesn't touch the water, combine the egg yolks, water and vinegar.

Check the temperature of the clarified butter with a thermometer—it should as close to 147°F as possible.

Set the bowl over the simmering water, ensuring the bottom of the bowl does not touch the water. Whisk vigorously until the mixture begins to foam and thickens noticeably. This will happen quickly. The temperature should be around 147°F. Continue to whisk, adding the clarified butter in a very thin stream until it is all incorporated. Remove from the heat and add salt to taste.

SERVES 4

3 large egg yolks
1½ Tbsp water
2 tsp rice wine or sherry vinegar
½ cup clarified butter (see sidebar)
   at 145°F–150°F
Salt

Clarified butter is very easy to make and is excellent to have on hand. Essentially, you are removing the milk solids and the water from the butter, creating an oil that has a higher smoking point than regular butter, as the milk solids are what causes butter to burn. Also, the shelf life will be a lot longer than that of regular butter because it's the milk solids that go rancid.

Gently melt 1 lb of unsalted butter (salted butter can behave in unexpected ways and you may not get the results you were hoping for) in a heavy-bottomed pan over low heat. You will see a layer of foam start to form at the top of the butter as it melts. Using a wide spoon, scrape this off and discard it (or better yet, save it to put it on your popcorn). Continue to scrape off the milk solids and foam, revealing a clear golden liquid below. Once all of the solids have been scraped off and all that is left is clear yellow liquid, pour the liquid butter into a clean airtight container and store in the refrigerator for up to 2 months.

Decisions, DECISIONS

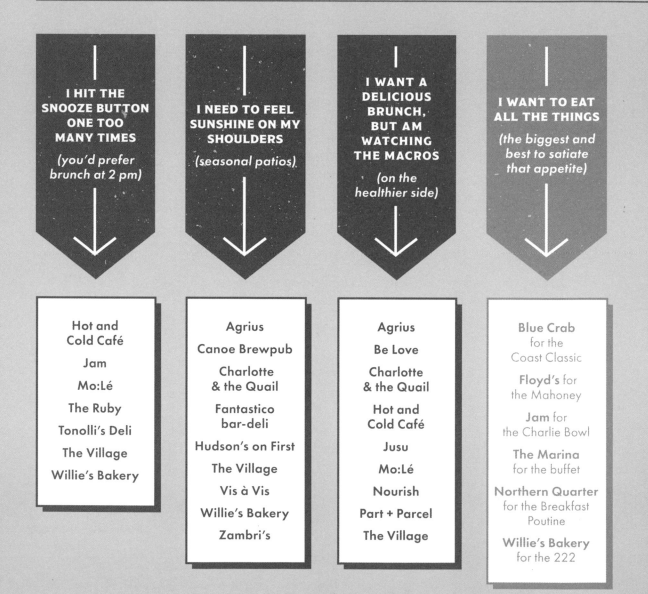

I HIT THE SNOOZE BUTTON ONE TOO MANY TIMES
(you'd prefer brunch at 2 pm)

Hot and Cold Café

Jam

Mo:Lé

The Ruby

Tonolli's Deli

The Village

Willie's Bakery

I NEED TO FEEL SUNSHINE ON MY SHOULDERS
(seasonal patios)

Agrius

Canoe Brewpub

Charlotte & the Quail

Fantastico bar-deli

Hudson's on First

The Village

Vis à Vis

Willie's Bakery

Zambri's

I WANT A DELICIOUS BRUNCH, BUT AM WATCHING THE MACROS
(on the healthier side)

Agrius

Be Love

Charlotte & the Quail

Hot and Cold Café

Jusu

Mo:Lé

Nourish

Part + Parcel

The Village

I WANT TO EAT ALL THE THINGS
(the biggest and best to satiate that appetite)

Blue Crab for the Coast Classic

Floyd's for the Mahoney

Jam for the Charlie Bowl

The Marina for the buffet

Northern Quarter for the Breakfast Poutine

Willie's Bakery for the 222

Where you're at in your day or your week, who you are with, and what you feel like eating will make the decision about where to go for brunch an important one. This is by no means an exhaustive list, but it will give you a few ideas based on those certain little factors.

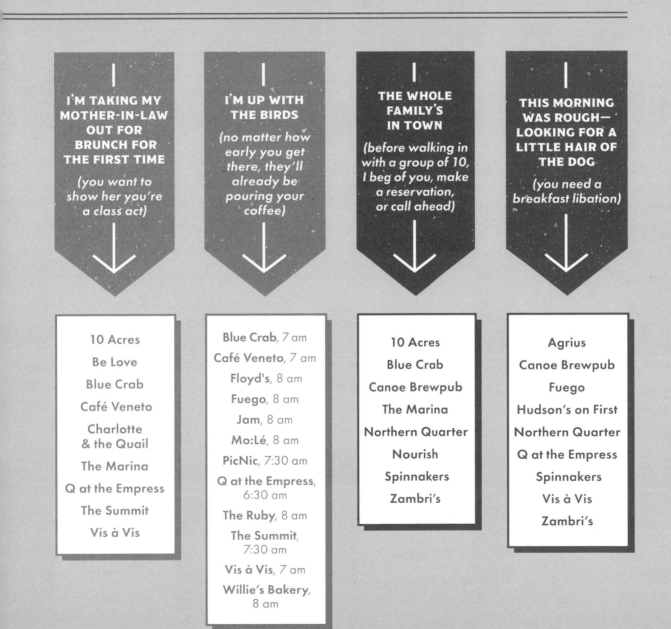

I'M TAKING MY MOTHER-IN-LAW OUT FOR BRUNCH FOR THE FIRST TIME

(you want to show her you're a class act)

↓

- 10 Acres
- Be Love
- Blue Crab
- Café Veneto
- Charlotte & the Quail
- The Marina
- Q at the Empress
- The Summit
- Vis à Vis

I'M UP WITH THE BIRDS

(no matter how early you get there, they'll already be pouring your coffee)

↓

- Blue Crab, 7 am
- Café Veneto, 7 am
- Floyd's, 8 am
- Fuego, 8 am
- Jam, 8 am
- Mo:Lé, 8 am
- PicNic, 7:30 am
- Q at the Empress, 6:30 am
- The Ruby, 8 am
- The Summit, 7:30 am
- Vis à Vis, 7 am
- Willie's Bakery, 8 am

THE WHOLE FAMILY'S IN TOWN

(before walking in with a group of 10, I beg of you, make a reservation, or call ahead)

↓

- 10 Acres
- Blue Crab
- Canoe Brewpub
- The Marina
- Northern Quarter
- Nourish
- Spinnakers
- Zambri's

THIS MORNING WAS ROUGH— LOOKING FOR A LITTLE HAIR OF THE DOG

(you need a breakfast libation)

↓

- Agrius
- Canoe Brewpub
- Fuego
- Hudson's on First
- Northern Quarter
- Q at the Empress
- Spinnakers
- Vis à Vis
- Zambri's

THE
BRUNCH
POTLUCK

It's possible that I choose my friends by how savvy they are in the kitchen—and it seems I have many friends who are rather exceptional cooks, bakers and cocktail makers. It is a common occurrence for us to gather, like many friends do, around a table laden with outstanding cocktails, good wine and meals to be remembered. We share newfound recipes, hash out the latest restaurant goings on and send group texts inquiring about where to find an obscure ingredient. There are discussions about food science (sourdough processes and cheese making and things infused) and making every little thing from scratch, because it's so much better, and who wouldn't take the time to brew their own tonic or make their own mustard or cure their own bacon? We have been known to feed each other across the table. In public.

It seems natural then, that every once in a while, we should crank some good tunes, brew extra coffee and mix brunch-appropriate cocktails, and all bring a dish or two to share. This is one of the best ways to eat, I'd say. Enthusiastic home cooks planning for days (and no kidding, sometimes weeks) and pulling out all the stops on a Sunday mid-morn. So, without further ado, I present to you: The Brunch Potluck.

Revive Brunch Smoothie

If you are hosting brunch, this is a great little healthy green start to drink while you're putting the finishing touches on the food.

In a high-speed blender, blend the grapes, orange, pineapple, banana, carrot, spinach, apple and ice cubes until smooth. Pour into individual cups and serve immediately.

1 cup washed, seedless red grapes
1 orange, peeled and quartered
1 cup fresh pineapple chunks
1 medium banana
1 medium carrot, scrubbed and trimmed
2 cups fresh baby spinach
1 apple, skin on and scrubbed, cored and quartered
5 cups ice cubes

Dutch Baby with Fruit Compote

This *Bon Appétit*–inspired pancake-like recipe puffs up like a soufflé, so it's important to serve it right out of the oven.

TO MAKE THE FRUIT COMPOTE

In a medium pot over medium-high heat, mix together the rhubarb, strawberries and sugar. Stir to blend the fruit with the sugar, then turn down the heat to medium-low. Stirring frequently so the mixture does not burn, allow to simmer for about 20 minutes, until the fruit has broken down into a chunky jam-like texture. Remove from the heat and set aside.

TO MAKE THE PANCAKE

Preheat the oven to 450°F.

In a large bowl, whip the cream with the icing sugar until it forms firm peaks. Set aside.

Place the butter in a 10-inch ovenproof frying pan (preferably cast iron). Put the frying pan in the oven to melt the butter, about 3 minutes. Remove from the oven and swirl to cover the entire bottom of the pan.

Blend the milk and eggs in a blender until smooth. Add the flour and salt and blend until just incorporated. Pour the batter into the hot frying pan, return to the oven and bake for about 11 minutes, or until the pancake is puffed and browned. Remove from the oven, top with the strawberry rhubarb compote and whipping cream and sprinkle icing sugar overtop through a sieve. Serve immediately.

Fruit Compote
2 cups chopped fresh rhubarb
1½ cups chopped fresh strawberries
2 tsp granulated sugar

Pancake
1 cup whipping (35%) cream
1 Tbsp icing sugar, plus more for garnish
3 Tbsp unsalted butter
¾ cup whole milk, at room temperature
3 large eggs, at room temperature
¾ cup all-purpose flour
Pinch of salt

Bourbon Mint Iced Tea

Why not enjoy a cocktail with brunch? There's no need to stop at pastries and cheese. After all, we are being indulgent.

½ cup granulated sugar
8 English Breakfast teabags
1 cup fresh mint leaves,
    plus more for garnish
2 cups bourbon
1–2 lemons
Ice cubes

In a large pot over high heat, bring 4 cups of water to a boil. Add the sugar and stir to dissolve. Remove from the heat and add the teabags. Let steep for 10 minutes and then discard the teabags. Chill for at least 1 hour.

When you are ready to serve, use a muddler or wooden spoon to muddle the mint in a pitcher until fragrant. Add the bourbon, the chilled tea and 4 cups cold water. Stir.

Squeeze the juice from one lemon into the mixture and taste. Add the juice from the second lemon to balance the sweetness as necessary. Serve over ice in rocks glasses and garnish with more mint.

When muddling mint, or any herb, it is important to be gentle. You don't want to bruise it, otherwise it will become bitter. Simply tap it and twist softly with the muddler or wooden spoon to release the essential oils.

Sausage and Smoked Cheddar Strata

Strata is one of my favourite brunch dishes and is extremely versatile. Use any herbs, vegetables and cheese in place of the ones suggested here. I highly recommend leaving it overnight if you can, as the bread will soak up all the ingredients, which allows the flavours to deepen.

Preheat the oven to 400°F.

If you are using dried shiitake mushrooms, place them in a large measuring cup and cover with boiling water. Let sit until the mushrooms are reconstituted, about 20 minutes. Remove from the water, squeeze out any excess moisture and chop.

Combine the butternut squash, shiitake mushrooms and olive oil and mix well. Season to taste with salt and pepper. Spread them in a single layer on a baking tray and roast in the oven for 25–30 minutes, or until the squash is tender. Remove from the oven, sprinkle with 1 Tbsp of the oregano and set aside.

In the meantime, remove the sausages from their casings. Place a large sauté pan over medium-high heat and crumble the sausage meat into the pan. Cook for about 10 minutes, until browned. Remove from the heat, drain the fat from the pan and set aside.

Mix together the eggs, half and half, the remaining 3 Tbsp oregano and salt and pepper to taste. Set aside.

Wipe out the sauté pan and heat about 1 tsp olive oil over medium-high heat. Add the kale and stir-fry for 2–3 minutes, until slightly wilted.

In a 3-quart buttered casserole dish, layer half the bread, half the kale, half the squash and mushroom mixture, half the sausage, and half the cheese. Repeat each layer, ending with the cheese on top. Pour the egg mixture evenly over the top. If possible, cover with plastic wrap and refrigerate overnight.

On the morning you are serving the strata, remove it from the fridge 20–30 minutes prior to baking. Preheat the oven to 350°F. Remove the plastic wrap, cover with aluminum foil and bake for 30–40 minutes, until the strata is firm in the middle when you touch it with your finger. Remove the foil and bake for another 10–15 minutes, or until the top is browned and a bit crispy. Let sit for 10 minutes before serving.

4 oz dried shiitake mushrooms, or 8 oz fresh shiitake mushrooms, chopped
1 small butternut squash, peeled, seeded and cut into ½-inch cubes
1 Tbsp extra virgin olive oil, plus more for frying
Salt and ground black pepper
4 Tbsp minced fresh oregano (or thyme or flat-leaf or curly parsley), divided
2 lb rosemary mushroom sausages (or your favourite flavour)
12 large eggs
2½ cups half and half cream (or whole milk)
1 bunch of kale, stiff stems discarded and leaves torn into pieces
Butter for greasing casserole dish
1 loaf of sourdough (about 1 lb), cut into 1-inch cubes
2½ cups grated smoked cheddar

Mount Royal Bagels with Spicy Smoked Salmon Spread

This is a fairly traditional way of serving bagels with lox. In this case, though, harissa, a North African hot chili pepper paste is added to the cream cheese, along with flaked salmon. It's nice to place all the toppings in small bowls to allow guests to build their bagels as they like!

TO MAKE THE SPICY SMOKED SALMON SPREAD

Drain (if using canned) and chop the salmon. Place it in a medium bowl. Add the garlic and capers. Using a sieve, rinse the onions under warm water for 30 seconds. This decreases their potency and prevents them from dominating the flavour of the spread. Shake the excess water from the onions and place them in the bowl with the salmon. Add the cream cheese, yogurt, lemon juice, dill, parsley and harissa. Using a fork, mix all the ingredients together until well blended. Season to taste with salt and pepper. This can be kept in an airtight container in the refrigerator for 2–3 days.

TO ASSEMBLE

Cut the bagels in half width-wise and place each half, cut side up, on a platter. Smear with some spicy smoked salmon spread. Top with lox, onion, capers, caper berries, radish slices and lemon slices. Garnish with watercress or other fresh herbs.

Spicy Smoked Salmon Spread

1 (6 oz) can flaked salmon
   or about ¾ cup freshly cooked
   and flaked salmon
2 garlic cloves, minced
2 Tbsp capers, chopped
¼ cup minced white or red onion
1 cup full-fat cream cheese, at room
   temperature, cut into small cubes
¼ cup plain full-fat yogurt
2 Tbsp fresh lemon juice
2 Tbsp finely chopped fresh dill
2 Tbsp finely chopped flat-leaf
   parsley
1 Tbsp harissa
Salt and ground black pepper

To assemble

4 bagels, any savoury flavour
4 oz lox
1 small red onion, thinly sliced
   into rings
3–4 Tbsp capers
½ cup caper berries
4 red radishes, sliced very thin
1 lemon, sliced very thin
Fresh watercress, dill or flat-leaf
   or curly parsley, for garnish

Sakura Maru Cocktail

This cocktail requires a bit more effort than some, but it's worth it. The green tea and yogurt make it certifiably brunch-appropriate. It makes sense to make the Genever and the agave syrup in larger amounts, as both of these will keep well in the refrigerator for about a month. Assemble two cocktails at a time, so all of the ingredients fit into your cocktail shaker, then repeat the process for more.

TO MAKE THE GREEN TEA-INFUSED GENEVER

In a jar or large measuring cup, add the green tea leaves to the Genever. Let infuse for 8–12 hours. Strain.

TO MAKE THE JASMINE TEA YOGURT

Steep the tea leaves in the boiling water for 5 minutes. Strain and discard the tea leaves. Add the sugar to the tea and stir until fully dissolved. Add the yogurt and stir until well incorporated. Let cool for about 15 minutes.

TO MAKE THE AGAVE SYRUP

Place the agave syrup and water in a small pot. Warm over medium heat until it starts to simmer. Remove from the heat and let cool for at least 30 minutes.

TO ASSEMBLE

Place the jasmine tea yogurt, lemon juice, Pisco, green tea–infused Genever, cachaça and agave syrup in a cocktail shaker. Add three ice cubes and shake vigorously until well blended and chilled. Pour over more ice in rocks glasses and garnish with orange or lemon slices.

Green Tea–Infused Genever
1 Tbsp Silk Road Sublime Green Tea leaves
1 cup Genever (if you can't find this, use London Dry gin)

Jasmine Tea Yogurt
1 Tbsp Silk Road Jasmine Oasis tea leaves
½ cup boiling water
½ cup granulated sugar
½ cup plain, full-fat yogurt

Agave Syrup
½ cup agave syrup
½ cup water

To assemble 2 cocktails
2 oz jasmine tea yogurt
1 ½ oz fresh lemon juice
1 ½ oz Pisco
1 ½ oz green tea–infused Genever
1 oz aged cachaça
½ oz agave syrup
Ice cubes
Dehydrated orange or lemon slices, for garnish (or fresh, thinly sliced if you don't have a dehydrator)

Spinach Quiche with Bacon

Individual quiches are great for potlucking. The foolproof whole wheat pastry recipe is from a local vegetarian restaurant in Bastion Square called Rebar. The bacon adds an excellent smoky flavour, though you can leave it out for a vegetarian option if preferred.

Whole Wheat Pastry
2 cups all-purpose flour
¾ cup whole wheat flour
½ tsp salt
½ tsp granulated sugar
½ cup vegetable shortening
6 Tbsp unsalted butter, chilled
½ cup ice water

Quiche
1 Tbsp unsalted butter
1 cup thinly sliced shallots
5 large eggs
1½ cups whipping (35%) cream
¾ tsp salt
⅛ tsp cayenne pepper
Pinch of ground nutmeg
1¼ cups grated Gruyère cheese
2 (each 10 oz) packages frozen chopped spinach, thawed and wrung completely free of water
5 slices maple rosemary bacon, cooked and crumbled

TO MAKE THE WHOLE WHEAT PASTRY

In a large bowl, place both flours, the salt and sugar and mix together. Add the shortening and butter. With your fingertips, mix carefully until the dry ingredients and the fats form a coarse meal. Sprinkle in the water and mix with your hands just until the dough holds together. Form it into two balls, cover each tightly with plastic wrap and refrigerate for 30 minutes, or up to 2 days.

Preheat the oven to 350°F.

Wipe the countertop with a slightly damp cloth and spread a large sheet of plastic wrap over the moistened surface. Smooth the plastic so there are no wrinkles. Place one ball of dough in the centre of the plastic and press down on it with your palm to make a 6-inch circle. Cover the dough with a second piece of plastic wrap. Roll out the dough in strokes, radiating from the centre, placing even pressure on the rolling pin. The dough should be about ¼ inch thick.

Remove the top piece of plastic from the dough, and, using a cutter (about 5 inches in diameter), cut out circles. Place each circle of dough into a muffin tin and press them firmly into place with your thumb, tucking and folding them to create a shell. The dough will shrink a bit when baked, so it should be slightly higher than the muffin tin. Prick the bottom and sides of the dough with a fork to prevent it from puffing up when pre-baking. Repeat with the second ball of dough. Bake the shells for 15 minutes, or until slightly golden. Keep an eye on them while baking and prick with a fork again if the dough starts to puff up.

Remove the shells from the oven and turn down the oven heat to 325°F.

TO MAKE THE QUICHE

Heat the butter in a small sauté pan over medium-low heat. Cook the shallots for 5–8 minutes, until soft and translucent, ensuring they don't brown. Set aside to cool.

In a medium bowl, whisk together the eggs, cream, salt, cayenne and nutmeg.

Spread the shallots over the bottom of the crusts, then sprinkle the Gruyère overtop. Scatter the spinach evenly over the cheese (breaking up any clumps), then pour the egg mixture overtop. Top with the crumbled bacon.

Bake for 45 minutes, until the custard is set and the top is lightly golden.

Grits with Beer-Braised Shrimp and Smoky Potatoes

There are layers and layers of flavours in this dish: smoky roasted potatoes, rich cheddar, sweet shrimp... This is fantastic for brunch, but can really be served at any meal. Our local Hoyne Pilsner provides great flavour for braising the shrimp.

TO MAKE THE GRITS

Bring 6 cups of water to a simmer in a large pot over medium-high heat. Gradually whisk in the grits. Turn down the heat to low and gently cook until the grits begin to thicken. Continue cooking, stirring often and adding water ¼ cup at a time if necessary, until the grits are tender and thick, about the consistency of mashed potatoes. This will take about 1 hour. Stir in the cheese and butter, then the jalapeños, then the cream. Season to taste with salt and pepper. Cover to keep warm.

TO MAKE THE SMOKY POTATOES

Preheat the oven to 425°F.

Toss the potatoes in a large bowl with the olive oil and both paprikas. Season to taste with salt and pepper. Place the potatoes on baking tray, and roast in the oven for 10–12 minutes, stirring occasionally, until crisp and golden. Remove from the oven and set aside.

TO MAKE THE BEER-BRAISED SHRIMP

Meanwhile, heat a large, heavy skillet over medium heat. Add the olive oil. Once it's warm, add the garlic and the butter. Stir until the butter melts. Add the shrimp. When the garlic begins to brown, add the beer and vegetable stock. Simmer for about 2 minutes, until the shrimp is opaque and cooked through. Remove the skillet from the heat and set aside.

Fry the eggs. (See page 185.)

Divide the grits evenly among eight bowls, forming a well in the centre. Spoon potatoes and shrimp into the centre of the grits. Place a fried egg on top of each bowl, and garnish with chives. Serve immediately.

Grits

2 cups yellow grits
2 cups grated aged white cheddar
2 Tbsp unsalted butter
2 jalapeño peppers,
    seeded and finely diced
½ cup half and half cream
Salt and ground black pepper

Smoky Potatoes

4 medium Yukon Gold potatoes,
    skins on, cut into ½-inch dice
2 Tbsp extra virgin olive oil
½ tsp smoked paprika
¼ tsp hot paprika
Salt and ground black pepper

Beer-Braised Shrimp

¼ cup extra virgin olive oil
6 garlic cloves, sliced
1 Tbsp unsalted butter
2 lb side stripe shrimp,
    peeled and deveined
½ cup pilsner beer
½ cup low-salt vegetable stock
8 large eggs
2 Tbsp chopped fresh chives

Where We Grab

BREAK FAST

ON THE GO

It's 10:30 on any day of the week.
You're running out the door to catch the
ferry/attend a meeting/meet a friend.
You're hungry. So, you stop at one of the
many places in town to grab a satiating,
savoury sandwich or a decadent sweet to
tide you over. Do we call this brunch? Let's.
At least for the purpose of this book.

These are the quick stops. The run ins.
The grab and gos.

The options and variety of breakfast grabs
in this town are endless.

CHARELLI'S
CHEESE SHOP AND DELICATESSEN

Charelli's offers so many good things—an impressive selection of cheeses, crackers, housewares, pastas, and an incredible array of high-quality canned, jarred, and fresh deli products. They also have a huge selection of bitters and shrubs, glassware, mixes, bar tools, syrups, garnishes and many other cocktail-related items. Ask them to create a custom gift basket for you, or to help plan and cater your event. They do both beautifully. It's a great shop to peruse, but be warned—if you're buying a gift for someone, you will almost certainly end up picking up something for yourself (or is that just me?).

Charelli's opens their little takeout window and offers up made-on-the-spot breakfast sandies. Choose from bacon, ham or chorizo (or a combo) and they will whip you up an omelette with cheese, add some fresh greens and Sun Wing tomatoes fresh from our island peninsula, and tuck it all into a steamed Portuguese bun from local Casa Nova Bakery. Pick up the makings of a well-rounded cheese plate, browse the latest local cookbooks and make sure you don't leave without a chinwag with the famous Charelli's Cheese Chicks!

CHARELLI'S CHEESE SHOP AND DELICATESSEN

2851 FOUL BAY ROAD

charellis.com →

250.598.4794

CRUST BAKERY

I don't have much of a sweet tooth. Bakeries aren't places I typically haunt, as I prefer the savoury flavours of warm cheesy things to sweet ones when I decide to indulge.

Crust, however, is one exception. It's a wonderful place to pick up treats when you would rather forego making them yourself. When I walked in there recently, I wasn't surprised to see the small space jam-packed with people pressing their fingers against the glass, pointing to their current need/want and inhaling the delectable smell of dough and crust and sugar in the air. The scene was like a bakery of old, with folks shouting their orders, a calm chaos behind the counter, money, boxes, and bags exchanging hands, satisfied looks on all faces. I scanned the sweets (and considered the Cronut, which I had heard was a must-have) and kept going until I saw them. There they were. A whole series of savouries, from quiches (zucchini, dill and feta! Mushroom, pine nut and goat cheese!) to croissants stuffed with bacon, tomato and cheese, to a bacon and egg Danish.

I left with six things that day, and I knew that the next time I needed a selection of beautiful pastries, Crust was where I would be, joining the masses, pressing my finger against the glass. And maybe that next time I'd also grab that Cronut.

CRUST BAKERY

730
FORT STREET

crustbakery.ca →

250.978.2253

DAK

Fort St. superstar couple Jon and Melissa Perkins run Dak, along with PicNic (page 132) and PicNic Too, found farther down and farther up Fort St. respectively. *Dak* is the Korean word for chicken and Korean-inspired rotisserie chicken is Dak's greatest specialty, featuring flavours such as sesame oil, ginger, garlic and gochu, a spicy Korean chili pepper. The Korean influence comes from the two years the couple spent teaching English in Korea. They brought back recipes for dishes such as the aforementioned roasted chicken, congee bowls with a Western twist and bop bowls made with steamed purple rice. Many other hints of Korean flavours and influences are found throughout their menu.

Their breakfast sandwich is laced with kimchi mayo, a tangy, slightly spicy sauce, on a sesame bun with avocado, sweet bacon, a fried egg and fresh greens. Have a seat at their long communal table, or at the window bar in the clean-lined tech building where Dak lives, right in the midst of Victoria's Fort Common's food district. Dak provides freshly baked goods daily and local 2% Jazz coffee, so with this combo, your morning is easily off to a great start.

DAK 838 FORT STREET
facebook.com/dakrotisserie

FERNWOOD COFFEE CO./ PARSONAGE CAFÉ

Fernwood Coffee Co./Parsonage Café is a little hot spot combining a well-established and innovative coffee company with a popular café full of all sorts of good things. Many a morning has found me there in pursuit of their amazing breakfast sandwich. The bagel is from Mount Royal (page 256), the bacon from Slater's and the egg from Farmer Ben's (page 248). Add cheese, fresh tomato and creamed spinach (my favourite part) and you have the ultimate morning pick-me-up for a quick or leisurely breakfast. The hardest part about going into Fernwood/Parsonage is choosing from their delicious selection of freshly created goods. Although 9 times out of 10 I end up with the breakfast sandwich, there are many choices, such as their new breakfast scone—a chive scone with prosciutto, aged cheddar and an egg baked right in—or a towering slice of freshly baked quiche to give but two examples. More often than not, I run into someone I know there. It is a destination for many, whether for a quick run in and out, or to hang out and catch up in the cozy booths.

Fernwood coffee is featured at many of our fine eateries around town, and recently I was introduced to Fernwood Coffee Cold Brew carbonated coffee—a surprisingly delicious, not-too-sweet, refreshing drink that is also available in many shops and markets.

FERNWOOD COFFEE CO./ PARSONAGE CAFÉ

1-1115
NORTH PARK STREET
fernwoodcoffee.com →
250.383.5999

FOL EPI

FOL EPI
101-398
HARBOUR ROAD
250.477.8882

732
YATES STREET
778.265.6312

→ folepi.ca →

Walking into Fol Epi is like walking into a bread and pastry lover's dream. Not only are both their locations beautiful spaces, but wherever possible their breads and other baked goods are made with locally sourced organic ingredients. Gorgeous tarts, pizzas, cookies, macarons, Danishes, sandwiches and breads of all types are made there. A great deal of care and love goes into the items made at Fol Epi—I am a long-time fan for good reason.

Cliff Leir is Fol Epi's creator and long-time baker, and I remember photographing him long ago in his makeshift bakery, in the midst of a construction site, while his first location was being built on Harbour Road. Even then, with the space restrictions and big demands, Cliff produced the most beautiful loaves in his wood-fired brick oven, delivering them to markets and restaurants all over town. Now, we make a point of going to him, and we are always glad we did.

Fol Epi's breakfast sandwich, like all the other treats, lives up to all its rave reviews. Whether you are downtown or in Vic West, stop at Fol Epi for a freshly baked and toasted ciabatta bun with a smiling sunny-side-up egg, a sharp slice of cheddar, some delicious back bacon and a tart and tasty tomato jam. Grab a few other treats while you're there, and if you catch a glimpse of Cliff, be sure to applaud him for his baking genius and all he brings to our bread-loving town.

THE ITALIAN BAKERY

It is customary in Italy to breakfast on espresso and pastry. Where better, then, to stop by than the Italian Bakery when you want to grab a creamy custard-filled brioche or a flaky, buttery croissant, or a breakfast sandwich for that matter?

As you listen to dramatic notes of Italian music in the background, you catch the wafts of freshly baked pizza, check out the homemade gelato and imagine swiping a finger through the tiramisù. Curly Italian words such as *cannoli* and *zuppa* and *campanelle* trip off your tongue as you read the lunch specials softly to yourself, and hey, why not order a cake while you're here, and grab a loaf of bread or two? Experienced chefs and fine Italian craftsmanship behind the counter since 1978 ensure quality and deliciousness and so yes, you decide to order the Chegger, their special asiago cheese bun and egg sandwich. The egg yolk oozes in between the swirls of crispy, soft cheese bun. The sweet caramel of the onions, the silkiness of the spinach and the salty prosciutto cotta (the best ham) mingle happily as you sip an espresso and think about your afternoon. Who feels like cooking? Not me. Grab a pan of lasagna made with house-made pasta to go and dinner (and probably lunch tomorrow, too) is taken care of.

THE ITALIAN BAKERY

3197 QUADRA STREET

italianbakeryvictoria.com

250.388.4557

JUSU BAR

800
YATES STREET
250.590.8724

513
FISGARD STREET
250.590.7077

2560B
SINCLAIR ROAD
250.590.8215

1965
OAK BAY AVENUE
778.265.8004

jusubar.com →

JUSU BAR

If you appreciate starting your day with some wholesome, healthful and delicious food, this is the place to be. With a menu full of whole, organic foods, juices, smoothies and elixirs, you will leave there at any time of day feeling utterly elevated and energized, knowing you've taken good care of yourself today.

Jusu comes with a big story—one that is too long to tell here, but know that it is both a tragic and a triumphant one. With an intense and focused desire to make the world a healthier place, a lovely man began Jusu here in Victoria, and it has since become a recognized and treasured destination around our town and beyond. Jusu's menu has expanded from their original juices, smoothies and elixirs to include beautiful soups, dips, sandwiches, smoothie bowls and, my favourite, wraps made with the pulp of the vegetables and fruits they juice. Most recently, Jusu has introduced a pulp-infused body care line of cleansers, moisturizers, scrubs and lip balms to name a few. Any one of Jusu's wraps, sandwiches, parfaits, mylks or juices makes a great start to your day, and for its beauty and energizing ingredients, the dragon fruit bowl is perfect for getting that hit of organic, wholesome and healthful.

MARINA DOCKSIDE EATERY

If you're the kind of person who likes to sit on a sun-soaked deck, gazing out onto a gorgeous sparkling marina, sipping on a latte (or a beer), then you should probably stop in at Marina Dockside Eatery. Living on an island has its advantages, and sitting waterside, enjoying the view is one of them. There is just something about being next to the ocean. The smells, the sounds and the fresh air are like nowhere else. We are so lucky here.

Marina Dockside Eatery is just a few steps away from The Marina Restaurant in Oak Bay and though their menus are very different, the Eatery also offers high-quality house-made dishes that contain exceptional ingredients. A much more casual, counter-service establishment than its counterpart restaurant, the Eatery is the perfect stop on a Sunday walk or bike ride. Definitely indulge in one of their selection of breakfast sandwiches—I particularly recommend the one made with a steamed egg, Swiss cheese, bacon, arugula, pickled onion and lemon aioli on a pretzel bun. This might be the best way to while the morning away until it's an appropriate time of day for a dish of gelato and a second latte.

MARINA DOCKSIDE EATERY

1327 BEACH DRIVE

marinadocksideeatery.com

250.598.3890

MOSI BAKERY

Stefano and Melissa Mosi, whom you may know from La Collina Bakery, run Mosi Bakery. With a family history of baking that goes back several generations, you can be sure these two are bringing us some wonderful fresh, delicious and beautiful baked goods.

Mosi Bakery is in a sweet little building out on West Saanich Rd., which makes it a great stop whenever you're heading anywhere up the Saanich peninsula. With a covered porch at the front, and a room full of breads, sweet and savoury croissants, stunning and gigantic meringues, pastries and countless other beauties, Mosi is a fabulous place to hang out or to drop in. Their breakfast menu goes far beyond a breakfast sandwich to say the least, with such items as the Sunrise Salad, several bennies, baked farro, and a Country Breakfast with Italian sausage.

If you are just popping in, I highly recommend the Veggie Bun on the Run. It's a freshly baked bun with fried egg, caciocavallo cheese, steamed kale, sundried tomato mayo and Mosi's fantastic romesco sauce. Be sure to grab a box of baked goodies before you go.

MOSI BAKERY

5303 WEST SAANICH ROAD

mosibakery.com

250.590.7969

RUTH & DEAN

You may recognize their name for the out-of-this-world cakes and pies they have been providing to many a celebratory table throughout town and beyond. To supplement their baking genius, Ruth and Dean (really, they are wife and husband Susannah Ruth and Robert Dean, plus Susannah's super-awesome brother thrown in for good measure) opened a wee luncheonette in 2015 to further share their talents and treats, both sweet and savoury.

Ruth and Dean offer a regularly rotating menu of lusty offerings featuring classy comfort food to perfectly match their cozy little space. Such things as shrimp and grits, broccoli and asiago grilled cheese, fish cakes and bánh mì show up as well as an often-changing soup feature. However, before you even start thinking about lunch, you must try their breakfast sandwich. The cheese scone that wraps itself lovingly around this breakfast sandwich is one of the very best scones I have ever tasted. I am a big fan of vegetable-type things in my sandwiches, and with fresh tomato, avocado and a killer chimichurri, this one hits the spot. You needn't skip the sweets, though. It should be noted, especially here, that cake for breakfast is still thoroughly acceptable, and is indeed encouraged.

RUTH & DEAN

1310
DOUGLAS STREET

⟶ ruthanddean.com ⟶

778.265.6060

Where We
SHOP

Despite the abundance of outstanding culinary delights we find outside our doors on a daily basis in Victoria, there are times when breakfast in bed seems appropriate and preferred. If you are feeling somewhat ambitious, or you are the planning-ahead type of human, there are several highly regarded shops in town to pick up the necessary supplies. The best part is that these folks also supply our fine restaurants and shops, contributing to the incredibly collaborative nature of this little city.
Pop by any of these places to grab meat, cheese, vegetables, bread and more.
And tell them all I say hello.

BOND BOND'S BAKERY

Several years ago, I helped run a popular, tiny restaurant in downtown Victoria called Devour. It was owned by a good friend and chef who made this fantastic food that drew people out of their meetings and cubicles every lunch hour to line up at the door. Each morning, when I arrived at work, I would pop out into the neighbourhood to gather any extra ingredients we needed for the day. I got to know the shop owners and other restaurateurs, stopping for a moment to trade stories, remark on the weekend's activities or speculate about the neighbourhood's latest development. In my memory, the streets were sunny and bustling, with everyone starting their day. Bond Bond's Bakery was just around the corner, and I would go there to collect the delicious baguettes we needed for our daily sandwiches. Bond Bond's was always busy, the room warm with the morning's baking, delectable scents wafting through. I always loved that part of my day, and still cherish the memories that only a tight-knit neighbourhood like that one can make.

BOND BOND'S BAKERY

1010
BLANSHARD STREET
— bondbondsbakery.com →
250.388.5377

Dried Fruit Focaccia

MAKES 8" ROUND LOAF

This focaccia is a sweeter version of the typical one, thanks to the raisins, cranberries, honey and orange zest. It is a perfect addition to a brunch potluck, or simply to have on hand for breakfast with a hot coffee. Like any bread, this takes some planning and an overnight rest in the refrigerator before baking. Substitute equal amounts of comparable fruits for the raisins and cranberries, such as chopped, dried apricots or dried blueberries. Both work well with the flavour of the orange zest.

Fruit
½ cup dried cranberries
½ cup raisins of your choice
1 cup hot tap water

Sponge
1 cup bread flour
¼ tsp fresh yeast (or ⅛ tsp active dry yeast)
¾ cup warm tap water

Final Dough
1½ cups bread flour
1½ tsp sea salt
½ tsp fresh yeast (or ¼ tsp active dry yeast)
1 tsp finely grated orange zest
½ cup reserved fruit water
1 Tbsp honey
2 Tbsp unsalted butter, at room temperature, cut into ½-inch dice
1 tsp cornmeal (optional)
All-purpose flour for sprinkling
1 egg, whisked together with 1 Tbsp water to make an egg wash
1 tsp raw pearl sugar (or turbinado sugar)

TO MAKE THE FRUIT

Place the fruit in a medium bowl and cover with the water to macerate at room temperature for 1 hour. Drain, pressing hard to remove as much liquid as possible, and reserve this fruit water to use in the dough. You should have a minimum of ½ cup liquid.

TO MAKE THE SPONGE

Combine the flour and yeast in a bowl with the water until the water is absorbed. Cover with plastic wrap and let rest at room temperature for 3–4 hours before proceeding with the final dough mixing.

TO MAKE THE FINAL DOUGH

In a stand mixer fitted with the bread hook attachment, combine the flour, salt, yeast and zest with the fruit water, honey, macerated fruit and sponge mixture on low speed for about 1 minute, until all the flour is absorbed. Increase the speed to medium and mix for 4 minutes to develop the dough strength. The dough will appear to be tacky in appearance—this is normal. With the machine still running, add the butter and mix for an additional 1–2 minutes, until the butter is fully blended into the dough. Leaving the dough in the mixer bowl, cover loosely with plastic wrap and leave to rest at room temperature for 2–3 hours.

Line the bottom of a 10- or 12-inch round baking pan with parchment paper and sprinkle it evenly with the cornmeal (if using). Sprinkle your countertop with a generous amount of all-purpose flour and scrape the dough out of the mixer and onto this floured surface. The dough will be quite tacky—again, this is normal for this type of dough. Quickly form the dough into a loose round. Place it in the baking pan and press it into a rough round about 8 inches in diameter. Sprinkle with a light dusting of flour, cover tightly with plastic wrap and refrigerate overnight.

DAY OF BAKING

Remove the bread dough from the fridge, but leave it in the baking pan. You can leave it covered with the plastic wrap or remove the wrap and instead cover it with a large bowl that fits right over the pan. Let the bread dough come to room temperature for its second and final rise prior to baking. This can take 3–4 hours, depending on the temperature of the room.

Once the dough has risen, and has preferably doubled in height from its refrigerated state, remove the cover and use your fingertips to dimple the dough surface.

Preheat the oven to 375°F.

Brush the dough gently with the egg wash to cover surface and then sprinkle with the raw sugar. Bake for 16 minutes, or longer if a darker crust is desired. Allow to cool slightly before slicing. This bread can be kept well wrapped in plastic at room temperature for 2 days or frozen in a freezer-safe bag for up to 1 month.

Bond Bond's recommends sprinkling the pans with a bit of cornmeal when making flat breads. It helps the dough release from the pan or parchment paper lining after baking, but it's not essential.

Swedish pearl sugar is a great addition for this bread as it looks like rock salt but has the added surprise of being sweet when you bite into it. It is, however, a specialty store item and you may have to seek it out online. It has a great shelf life, though, and it can be used in many fun baking applications, so it's worth the effort of tracking it down.

FARM + FIELD BUTCHERS

Here is what I love about Farm + Field: Not only do they carry ethically raised and locally farmed products, but also, thanks to them, I'm off the hook when I can't find the time to make my own ragu sauce or beef broth or duck fat. Their fridges, freezers and shelves are full of beautifully concocted house-made products that allow us all to indulge without spending hours in the kitchen.

Rebecca Teskey, whom I like not only because of her stellar name, is the mastermind behind Farm + Field, with a strong team of talented, cleaver-wielding guys behind her, who always have a good suggestion for the best cut or technique, or a recipe or two. The bright and clean shop is in the Fort Common district, making it easy to grab a coffee from Discovery just next door, stop in for a juice at Be Love (page 24) or pick up a loaf from Bond Bond's Bakery (page 236) across the street. Here, I want to introduce you to their sausages. With such flavours as rosemary and mushroom, and plum and brandy, the range is suitable for breakfast, barbecue or any other occasion you can think of. I created a recipe with their chorizo because sometimes, when simple is done just right, it's really all you need.

FARM + FIELD BUTCHERS

1003
BLANSHARD STREET
farmandfieldbutchers.com
250.415.8373

Huevos Rancheros con Chorizo

Huevos rancheros, which is Spanish for "rancher's eggs," is one of my favourite brunch dishes. This recipe has lots of steps, but trust me, it's worth it. I highly recommend making the beans and salsa macha at least a day ahead. Or feel free to purchase some of the components instead, if time is not on your side. There are many versions of salsa macha, but I like this one by Pati Jinich.

TO MAKE THE SALSA MACHA

In a large wok or heavy frying pan, heat the olive oil until hot but not smoking. Add the garlic, and stir constantly for about 1 minute, until the cloves are slightly browned. With hot oil, things can cook quickly, so keep your eye on the heat and keep stirring. Add the chilies and peanuts and stir-fry for about 2 minutes, or until they start to become fragrant. Add the sesame seeds, stirring for about 1 minute more. Remove from the heat, and then carefully transfer all of the contents to a blender. Let cool in the blender for about 10 minutes. Add the vinegar, sugar and salt and blend all the ingredients well, until the mixture is kind of smooth, but still with a little texture. This makes 1¾ cups, which is more than you need for this recipe, so pour it into an airtight jar and store it in the refrigerator for up to 3 months.

TO MAKE THE REFRIED BEANS

Add the olive oil to a large pot over medium-high heat. Add the onion, and cook for 5–7 minutes, stirring, until softened but not browned. Add the garlic and cook for another minute. Add the cumin, chili powder and salt and stir for 1 minute. Add the pinto beans and stir to combine. Add the chicken stock or water, bring the mixture to a boil and then immediately turn down the heat to a simmer. Using the back of a spoon, or a potato masher, mash the beans into the liquid, continuing to cook, stir and mash for 10–15 minutes, until most of the liquid has cooked away and the beans are mashed to your desired texture. Stir in 3 Tbsp of the salsa macha. Remove from the heat and stir in the lime juice. Adjust the salt to taste. If you don't use all the beans in this dish, they can be stored in an airtight container in the refrigerator for up to 5 days or in the freezer for up to 3 months.

TO ASSEMBLE

Remove the chorizo from its casings and crumble the meat into a frying pan over medium-high heat. Fry until cooked through, about 10 minutes, and set aside in the pan to keep warm.

Salsa Macha

1¼ cups extra virgin olive oil
3 large whole garlic cloves
1 oz dried chipotle chilies, seeded, stemmed and torn into pieces (⅓ – ½ cup)
¼ cup raw, unsalted peanuts
1 Tbsp sesame seeds
2 Tbsp white vinegar
1 Tbsp brown sugar
½ tsp kosher salt

You can use any mild to medium dried chili that you prefer. Make sure to use the sundried type, not the type that are so dried that you can grind them into a powder. If you use something other than chipotle, add about 1 Tbsp of chipotle peppers in adobo sauce and a pinch of smoked paprika to get that essential smoky flavour.

Refried Beans

2 Tbsp extra virgin olive oil
1 medium yellow onion, finely diced
2 garlic cloves, minced
1 Tbsp ground cumin
1 tsp chili powder
1 tsp kosher salt
1 (19 oz) can pinto beans, drained and rinsed
¾ cup chicken stock or water
2 Tbsp fresh lime juice

Mix the tomato and onion together in a small bowl. Add vinegar, season with salt and pepper and set aside.

Heat a large cast iron pan over medium heat. One at a time, place a tortilla in the pan, and cook, watching closely, for 1–2 minutes per side, until just browned. Place each tortilla on a warm plate and top with about 3 Tbsp of refried beans. Divide the chorizo evenly between the four tortillas and arrange fresh arugula, avocado, tomato and onion, and queso fresco on top. Fry the eggs (see page 185), place one on top of each tortilla, garnish with cilantro and more salsa macha, if desired, and serve immediately.

To assemble

3 Farm + Field Butchers
    chorizo sausages
1 medium tomato, finely diced
1 small yellow onion, finely diced
2 tsp white vinegar
Salt and ground black pepper
4 (7-inch) flour or corn tortillas
About 2 cups fresh arugula
1 avocado, sliced
4 oz queso fresco
    (or crumbled feta cheese)
4 large eggs
Cilantro, for garnish

FARMER BEN'S EGGS

When I went out to visit Farmer Ben's Eggs in the Cowichan Valley, I didn't expect to actually meet the man himself. Ben is a lovely retired gentleman who built a thriving business, now run by his son Ian and daughter-in-law Jen. You can see Ben in the photo here with his tractor—maybe he's not completely ready to let go of the daily duties just yet.

Besides the typical urban chicken setup, or small production farm, I'd never been to see a real egg farmer, so I wasn't sure what to expect when I arrived. What I found were thousands of beautiful chickens. Happy, healthy and well loved, these ladies have been producing eggs that have been distributed all over Vancouver Island for over 40 years. As I learned more about the farm and business, I became more interested in the daily processes and hard work required to run a successful egg farm. The whole Woike family is fully hands-on at the farm and heavily involved in their Cowichan Valley community. Farmer Ben's supplies eggs to school breakfast programs, local food banks and the annual Heart and Stroke Foundation breakfast.

Plenty of the restaurants in this book serve Farmer Ben's eggs, and they are sold at a number of grocery stores and markets for you to take home and cook up yourself.

FARMER BEN'S EGGS

1711
HERD RD., DUNCAN BC
farmerbenseggs.ca →
250.746.6110

Bacon and Egg Brunch Caesar Salad

> I am a big fan of salad in the morning. This Caesar salad is amped up with bacon and eggs, making it perfect for big groups or potlucks. Make the dressing the night before and dress the salad just before serving.

In a large measuring cup, whisk together the egg yolks, garlic, vinegar, lemon juice and Worcestershire sauce. Very slowly, whisking constantly, drizzle in the olive oil until it is all incorporated and emulsified. Add the salt and pepper and refrigerate the vinaigrette in an airtight container for at least 4 hours. (The dressing should be used within a couple of days.).

Preheat the oven to 350°F.

In a large sauté pan, melt the butter over medium heat and add the bread cubes. Toss them around for 5–7 minutes, until the bread is coated with butter and beginning to brown. Remove from the heat and add the herbs. Toss to coat. Pour the contents of the pan onto a baking tray and bake for about 15 minutes, tossing once or twice to avoid burning, until the bread is crisp. Let cool for 10 minutes or so.

Place the greens in a large bowl. Add as much dressing as you like and toss well to coat. Chop the hard-boiled eggs and add them to the bowl along with the bacon, Parmesan and croutons. Season to taste with salt and pepper and serve immediately. (You can serve this with the bacon and eggs warm or cold, but you must serve it as soon as the dressing goes on so it doesn't go soggy.)

2 large Farmer Ben's egg yolks
2 garlic cloves, minced
2 Tbsp red wine vinegar
1 Tbsp fresh lemon juice
1½ tsp Worcestershire sauce
½ cup good extra virgin olive oil
¼ tsp sea salt
⅛ tsp ground black pepper
¼ cup unsalted butter
3 thick slices French bread,
    cut into 1-inch cubes
1 Tbsp minced fresh herbs
    (thyme or rosemary work well)
2 heads of romaine lettuce,
    or other greens such as baby
    spinach or kale, washed and
    torn into bite-size pieces
    (about 8 cups of greens)
4 hard-boiled eggs (see page 184)
6 strips bacon, cooked
    and crumbled
⅓ cup shaved Parmesan cheese

FINEST AT SEA

In February of 2016, I was fortunate enough to go out to the docks with the folks at Finest at Sea to welcome and photograph their first halibut boat of the season into the Victoria harbour. Watching the crew pull the giant fishes out of the boat and ready them for distribution around the city was amazing, and it was an honour to witness just a tiny part of the hard work and tough conditions that these guys endure to bring their quality products to our island. I could imagine the specials that would hit the plates that night, chefs enthusiastically anticipating the arrival of halibut season, reservations made all around the city, wine chosen and chilling to accompany the dishes. Another successful haul, with Finest at Sea bringing us the freshest of the fresh. And this is what they have been doing since 1977. Finest at Sea products can be found in countless restaurants around town, and their little boutique has all the best things ready for us to take home for weekend breakfast: everything from fresh oysters and crabs to smoked tuna and sablefish to delicious Coho salmon fill the display cases. Ready-made seafood delicacies are also available, along with a selection of books, canned goods and, just outside, their famous FAS food cart.

FINEST AT SEA

27
ERIE STREET
→ finestatsea.com →
250.383.7760

Salmon Wellingtons

SERVES 4

Who says you have to eat eggs for breakfast? These delicious salmon wellingtons are the perfect West Coast comfort brunch. This dish goes great with a little side of greens or, if you're feeling extra indulgent, a drizzle of hollandaise (see page 189). If you can't find Coho, any in-season salmon will do.

1 Tbsp extra virgin olive oil
1 Tbsp unsalted butter
10 leeks, sliced and washed
2 cups whipping (35%) cream
2 tsp fresh thyme leaves
Salt and ground black pepper
4 (each 4 oz) portions skin-off, deboned, Finest at Sea Coho salmon
4 sheets phyllo pastry
2–3 Tbsp salted butter, melted
⅓ cup curly parsley, finely chopped

Heat a large frying pan over medium heat. Add the olive oil and the unsalted butter and then the leeks, and sauté for 15–20 minutes, until cooked through. Turn down the heat and slowly add the cream, stirring constantly. Continue to cook, stirring frequently, for about 5 minutes, until the cream is well incorporated and has slightly reduced to create a thick mixture, and the leeks are thoroughly coated. Add the thyme and season to taste with salt and pepper. Remove from the heat, set aside and let cool.

Preheat the oven to 350°F. Line a sheet pan with parchment paper.

Season the salmon with salt and pepper.

Place a large piece of parchment paper in front of you on the counter. Lay one sheet of phyllo pastry on top of it, with a narrow end facing you. Fold down the top third of the phyllo and fold up the bottom third to make a triple layer of pastry.

Carefully brush the entire sheet with melted butter. Lay ¼ of the leeks in the centre of the pastry. Place the salmon on top of the leeks and fold the parchment over the salmon, tucking the edges in like a parcel and brushing with butter to help seal it. Flip the parcel over so the folds are at the bottom and gently set it on the prepared sheet pan. Repeat with the remaining pastry, leeks and salmon. Brush the top of each parcel with melted butter.

Bake for 20–25 minutes, or until the phyllo is lightly browned. Remove from the oven and arrange on four serving plates. Sprinkle a small amount of parsley on top of each piece. Let sit for 5 minutes before serving.

MOUNT ROYAL BAGEL FACTORY

Bagels are most definitely a brunch staple. Mount Royal Bagel Factory has been around since 1992, providing some top breakfast restaurants and shops with their bagels. They also run a little retail shop in the North Park area so folks like you and me can grab a sack of bagels to take home. They even sell a variety of flavours of cream cheese to go with them. A bagel with cream cheese, lox, red onion and capers is one of my favourite breakfasts and if you add an egg it's even better. Or go another route, with something a little less traditional, with some caramelization, creamy brie and smoky bacon.

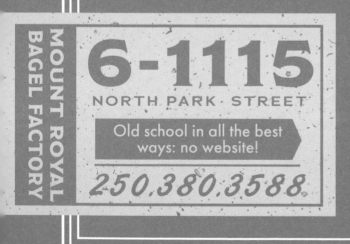

MOUNT ROYAL BAGEL FACTORY

6-1115
NORTH PARK · STREET

Old school in all the best ways: no website!

250.380.3588

Caramelized Pear, Bacon and Brie Bagel Sandwiches

This may seem like overkill for a sandwich, but I can promise you that having caramelized onions on hand at all times is a good idea. Double, or even triple, the caramelized onion step to ensure you have enough for future sandwiches! They will keep in an airtight container for about 4 days in the refrigerator or up to 3 months in the freezer.

2 Tbsp salted butter, divided,
   plus more for spreading
1½ tsp extra virgin olive oil, divided
1 large sweet onion, thinly sliced
1 Tbsp balsamic vinegar
3 tsp brown sugar, divided
1 tsp minced fresh thyme leaves
Salt and ground black pepper
1 large, ripe but firm pear, peeled,
   cored and sliced
1 cup fresh arugula
2 Mount Royal bagels,
   any savoury flavour, cut in half
5 oz brie, sliced
2 slices bacon, cooked
   and cut in half
2 large eggs

Heat 1 Tbsp of the butter and 1 tsp of the olive oil in a frying pan over medium-high heat. Add the onions, and cook, stirring frequently, for about 20 minutes, until browned and softened. Add the balsamic vinegar and 1 tsp of the brown sugar. Continue to cook, stirring frequently, for another 5–10 minutes, until the onions are further softened. Add the thyme and salt and pepper to taste. Remove from the heat and transfer to a bowl. Wipe out the frying pan.

Add the remaining 1 Tbsp butter to the frying pan over medium heat. Once it's melted, add the remaining 2 tsp brown sugar and let cook, stirring, for 1–2 minutes, until the mixture is bubbling slightly, taking care not to let it burn. Add the pear and let cook for 4–5 minutes, or until brown and caramelized. Flip the pear pieces over and cook for an additional 4 minutes, until browned on the second side. Remove from the heat, and transfer to a separate bowl. Wipe out the frying pan again.

Preheat the oven to 350°F.

Add the remaining ½ tsp olive oil to the pan over medium-low heat. Add the arugula to the pan and stir for 30–60 seconds, just until slightly wilted. Remove from the heat and transfer to a separate bowl.

Butter the cut sides of the bagels and place them cut side up on a sheet pan. Place the brie on the bottom halves of the bagels and bake for about 4 minutes, until the cheese is melted and the bagels are slightly toasted. Remove from the oven. Set a bottom bagel half on each of two plates. Drape bacon over the brie. Place half of the caramelized onions on top of each bagel, followed by pear slices and arugula. Fry the eggs. (See page 185.) Place an egg on top of each sandwich and cover with the bagel tops. Serve immediately.

ORIGIN BAKERY

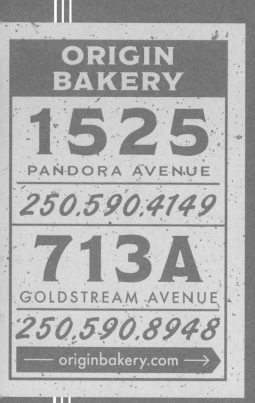

ORIGIN BAKERY

1525
PANDORA AVENUE

250.590.4149

713A
GOLDSTREAM AVENUE

250.590.8948

originbakery.com →

I can't remember the first time I met the two lovely ladies who run Origin Bakery, but I have worked with them a number of times over the years. Having photographed their gorgeous and exceptionally delicious gluten-free goods for multiple projects and publications, I am reminded every time I see them why I like them so much (and it's not only for their food). Super down to earth, these two bring gluten-free to a whole new level. Their products can be found at many restaurants, and are a popular gluten-free choice in town not only for the classic items such as bread, buns and muffins, but also for some impressive treats such as birthday and wedding cakes, marshmallows, pizzas and pies. Walking into Origin Bakery is a treat for the senses—baking scents wafting throughout, tempting, enticing and eye-catching. Icing and chocolate and berries are lathered and spread and distributed. Things are kneaded and stirred, whether for a wholesale delivery, a special order or a single purchase. It is clear that love and care go into every piece. Visit them in town or in Langford, to check out their frequently changing array of sweets and savouries.

Gluten-Free Cheese Scones

MAKES
12
SCONES

> It is worth doubling the batch when making these scones. They freeze well and are perfect for grabbing one at a time when you need a quick breakfast.

Preheat the oven to 375°F. Line a baking sheet with parchment paper.

In a large mixing bowl, whisk together the three flours, xanthan gum, baking powder, baking soda and salt. Dip one end of the butter into the flour mixture (this helps it grate more evenly) and grate the butter directly into the flour mixture. Toss the grated butter gently, using a rubber spatula, to distribute it evenly in the flour. Add the parsley and then the cheese into the flour mix.

In a large measuring cup, mix together the cream and honey. Pour this cream mixture into the dry mixture, and immediately mix together with a rubber spatula. Do not overmix, as this will make the scones tough. Using a large spoon, distribute the batter into 12 evenly sized mounds on the prepared baking sheet. Gently press each mound with the palm of your hand. Sprinkle the top of each scone with a bit of flaked salt.

Bake in the centre of the oven for 15–18 minutes, or until the outsides are golden brown. These last very well in the freezer in a freezer bag for up to 3 months. Bring to room temperature and then warm them in a 350°F oven for about 7 minutes.

1¾ cups sorghum flour
¾ cup + 1 Tbsp amaranth flour
1 cup tapioca flour
¼ tsp xanthan gum
1 Tbsp baking powder
½ tsp baking soda
½ tsp sea salt
½ cup unsalted butter, chilled
1 Tbsp finely chopped fresh flat-leaf parsley
1¼ cups shredded sharp white cheddar
1⅓ cups light (5%) cream
¼ cup honey
Flaked salt for sprinkling

OTTAVIO
ITALIAN BAKERY AND DELICATESSEN

Truly a family-style shop, Ottavio has long been my go-to for cheeses, olives, specialty grocery items, olive oils and baked treats. Not to mention a sandwich made with their house-made bread and a side of gelato for good luck. Oh, and an espresso to go. Just so you know, Ottavio has it all and then some.

The bakery and deli sits at the south end of Oak Bay Village, making it the perfect stop after a stroll through the shops along the avenue. Sit outside on their patio for a breath of fresh air and a bowl of house-made soup, or pick up some freshly made dough for pizza, a loaf of bread with some cheese and olives or a ready-made entrée to take home. If you are looking for some high-quality preserves, canned goods, dry pastas and grains and many other items and gifts, Ottavio is the place to go. Over the years, I have gotten to know and love the Ottavio folks, sharing their love for simple and beautiful food, attending their workshops and events (such as olive oil and cheese tasting) and simply enjoying their products and space here in our lovely city.

OTTAVIO
ITALIAN BAKERY
AND DELICATESSEN

2272
OAK BAY AVENUE
— ottaviovictoria.com →
250.592.4080

Bagnetto Verde

I am so honoured that Monica, Ottavio's co-owner, shared this family recipe with us to add to our brunch table. It is her maternal grandmother's (nonna Albertina) and great-grandmother's (bisnonna Teresa) recipe, and is from the Piedmont region of Italy. Traditionally, Monica's family eats it with roast meats, *bollito misto* (a classic northern Italian stew), roasted peppers or simply with bread. Hard-boiled eggs, cheese (especially fresh or young cheeses) and cured meats such as prosciutto are also the perfect accompaniment. Monica recommends that you use Agostino Recca anchovies for this versatile sauce.

1 slice of day-old white bread
1 ½ Tbsp red wine vinegar
2 bunches of flat-leaf parsley
3–4 anchovy fillets packed in olive oil
1 ½ Tbsp capers
1 cup extra virgin olive oil
3 whole garlic cloves

Break the bread up into medium-sized chunks in a small bowl and pour the vinegar overtop. Remove the stems from the parsley and clean the leaves thoroughly, using a salad spinner to drain the water.

Place as many handfuls of the parley leaves as will fit in your food processor and pulse, adding more parsley as the volume decreases and the parsley is well chopped. Remove the bread from the vinegar and squeeze it to remove any excess. It should be wet but not drippy.

With the food processor off, add the anchovies, capers and bread. Turn on the machine and blend well so you no longer see chunks of bread and everything is well incorporated. With the food processor running, slowly pour in the olive oil until the mixture is oily, but not runny. You may not need all the oil.

Transfer the mixture to a small airtight container and add the garlic cloves. Keep them whole, as you want to be able to remove them eventually.

Though you can eat the sauce immediately, it will last in the refrigerator for a week. Be sure to let it come to room temperature before eating it, as the olive oil will solidify in the refrigerator. Leave the garlic in for at least a day and taste it. When the garlic flavour begins to get too intense for you, you can remove it.

THE ROOT CELLAR
VILLAGE GREEN GROCER

I have this thing for grocery stores. They are my foodie playground. An amusement park of sorts with a vast variety of smells, tastes and colours. While I often shop visually for ingredients to style for a photo shoot, I also consider myself a home chef and I appreciate all that I can find on our little island and beyond. I enjoy perusing the cheeses and deli items, the bins of grains and nuts and seeds, the gigantic bins of apples and pears and five different kinds of every type of produce you can imagine. Maybe it's my penchant for all things that lend themselves to a beautiful image, or perhaps it's an expression of the pride and gratitude that comes from living in a part of the world that supports so many amazing food species. In any case, I find visiting The Root Cellar a fantastic experience, and over the years, as I've watched them grow, it has become even more of a pleasure to hang out . . . er . . . to shop there.

The Root Cellar's space is thoughtful and beautiful, and it's clear that they are conscious of maintaining a local focus with as many of their items as possible. And here's the thing. You can go into The Root Cellar with 167 thoughts on brunch, and actually find everything you need. While you're shopping, enjoy the local live music, be sure to try their custom Green Sauce (seriously), and for crying out loud, as The Root Cellar boldly asks, "Eat Your $%^& Vegetables, Please."

THE ROOT CELLAR

1286 McKENZIE AVENUE

therootcellar.ca →

250.477.9495

Black Quinoa Brunch Bowls

Quinoa is easy to cook, very nutritious, and delicious in many dishes. The most common types on the market today are white quinoa, black quinoa and red quinoa. White quinoa cooks up a bit fluffier, while black and red are a bit firmer with a toasty flavour. They all have the same cooking method—a 1:2 ratio of seeds to water and 15–20 minutes of cooking time. Any colour will work well in a brunch bowl.

The sauce is an adaptation of a recipe from the Hollyhock Institute, a lovely retreat centre on Cortes Island, just east of Vancouver Island. It's an excellent addition to any brunch bowl, salad or simple bowl of rice. I also use this recipe to marinate chicken before roasting or grilling. It is quite flavourful, and it goes well with milder brunch bowl components such as sautéed kale, avocado, pea shoots, poached eggs, green onions and deep-fried sun choke chips.

Once you've made these majestic bowls, it's easy to see how you could really add anything to them. The hard part is deciding what, exactly. Make a pot of quinoa (or use another grain if you prefer, such as brown rice, farro or wheat berries), add a sauce and some different textures, colours and herbs—and there you have it. Get creative!

Black Quinoa
1½ cups black quinoa
3 cups water
½ tsp kosher salt

Roasted Tofu
1 (14 oz) package firm organic tofu
1 garlic clove, minced
2 Tbsp toasted sesame oil
2 Tbsp tamari or soy sauce
2 Tbsp fish sauce
1 Tbsp mirin
1 Tbsp fresh lime juice

Nutritional Yeast Dressing
1 garlic clove
½ cup nutritional yeast flakes
⅓ cup tamari
⅓ cup apple cider vinegar
1 cup extra virgin olive oil

To assemble
Assorted vegetables

TO MAKE THE QUINOA

In a fine-mesh sieve, rinse the quinoa well with cold water.

In a medium pot over high heat, combine the quinoa, water and salt and bring to a boil. Turn down the heat to a simmer, cover and let cook for 15–20 minutes, or until the quinoa is fluffy and all of the water has been absorbed. Let the quinoa sit in the pot, covered, for 15 minutes, then fluff with a fork and dress as desired.

TO MAKE THE ROASTED TOFU

Cut the tofu into eight evenly sized rectangles.

Combine the garlic, sesame oil, tamari, fish sauce, mirin and lime juice in a bowl. Toss the tofu gently in this marinade. Cover and refrigerate for at least 3 hours, or up to overnight. Toss, turn or stir occasionally.

Preheat the oven to 400°F. Line a baking tray with parchment paper.

Remove the tofu from the marinade, pat lightly with paper towel and then place it on the prepared baking sheet. Roast for about 40 minutes, until the tofu is sizzling and slightly firm and has a nice brown colour.

TO MAKE THE NUTRITIONAL YEAST DRESSING

In a miniature food processor, pulse the garlic until minced. Add the nutritional yeast, tamari and apple cider vinegar, and pulse to blend. With the blender running, slowly drizzle in the oil until the sauce is thick and creamy. This dressing will keep in an airtight container in the refrigerator for several days.

TO ASSEMBLE

Add the nutritional yeast dressing to the quinoa (or try another dressing such as The Root Cellar's incredible Secret Green Sauce, Little Creek's Okanagan Original dressing, or The Stubborn Chef's Ginger Dressing).

Add assorted vegetables such as shredded carrots, avocados, green onions, sauerkraut, sautéed kale, spinach, roasted tomatoes, pickled onions, deep-fried sun choke chips or Christina's Garden Pea Shoot Greens.

Add the roasted tofu (or another protein such as The Root Cellar's custom-made Black Forest Bacon by Glenwood Meats, roasted chickpeas, or a variety of Root Cellar house-made sausages). Top with fried, boiled, scrambled or poached eggs (see page 182).

SILK ROAD TEA

I feel a great sense of community pride knowing that Silk Road Tea started in Victoria's Chinatown. I love to watch local businesses thrive, expand and spread their products, knowledge and philosophy far and wide. Silk Road not only produces and distributes organic, premium-quality teas, they also blend their own body care products. I am very fond of these products, especially when used in their organic spa, tucked just under the stairs in their charming Chinatown space. Silk Road brings us clean, pure, unadulterated things to put in and on our bodies, and also teaches us about the differences between certain tea leaves, their steeping time and how to incorporate them into food pairings, cocktails and frozen tea treats. The Silk Road Tea store is in a historic building, with a huge amount of character, and sells the most beautiful selection of cups, teapots and gift items and, of course, a vast array of teas and body care products.

You will find Silk Road teas at many restaurants and shops around town, or you can stop in at the shop to inquire about a tea tasting and to pick up any of their lovely products.

SILK ROAD TEA

1624 GOVERNMENT STREET

In the Victoria Public Market
6-1701 DOUGLAS STREET

silkroadteastore.com

250.382.0006 778-433-9838

Chai Maple Oatmeal

SERVES 4

> Chai is typically sold as a black tea, but herbal options are available at Silk Road. This recipe is vegan, dairy-free and gluten-free (make sure you are purchasing gluten-free oats if you want to avoid gluten completely). Omit the pecans to make it nut-free.

¼ cup Silk Road Chai
  or Herbal Chai leaves
4–5 cups unsweetened coconut milk
  (the kind in the carton, not the can)
1 tsp sea salt
4 cups rolled oats
¼ cup crushed pecans
1 cup canned coconut cream
Maple syrup, for garnish
Whole toasted pecans, for garnish

Bring 4 cups of water to a full rolling boil in a large pot over high heat. Add the tea. Steep for 10 minutes and strain the liquid into a large measuring cup. The tea leaves will absorb some of the water, so the volume of brewed tea may vary. Pour coconut milk into the measuring cup until you have a total of 8 cups.

Pour the coconut milk/tea mixture back into the large pot over medium-high heat. Add the salt. Stir with a wooden spoon. Bring the tea mixture to a boil, and then add the rolled oats and crushed pecans. Return the mixture to a boil for a brief moment, then immediately turn down the heat to low and simmer for 10–20 minutes, depending on your preferred consistency for oats (a longer cooking time results in creamier oats; a shorter cooking time means the oats will have more texture to them). Stir occasionally, and keep a close eye on the oatmeal so that it doesn't burn. When the oatmeal reaches your desired texture, turn the heat off.

Divide the oatmeal between four warm bowls. Garnish with a dollop or two of coconut cream, maple syrup to taste and whole pecans.

The coconut milk that comes from a carton is a lighter, less rich version than the one that comes from a can and its consistency works well to cook the oats in. The thicker, more condensed canned coconut cream is perfect for a creamy topping to dollop before serving.

Silk Road's flagship store is in Victoria's historic Chinatown, and there are two smaller stores in the Hudson Market and on West 4th Ave. in Vancouver. Victoria's Chinatown is the oldest Chinatown west of the Great Lakes, and it hosts a few blocks full of grocery stores, galleries, teahouses and specialty shops. It's definitely worth a visit. Get lost in Fan Tan Alley and all the other nooks and crannies around the area.

THE WHOLE BEAST
ARTISAN SALUMERIA

Chef Cory Pelan (a self-proclaimed meat nerd) opened his little Oak Bay shop in 2011, combining his passion for butchery with a supreme knowledge of how to create the wonderful selection of ever-changing sausages, charcuterie and hand-crafted cured meats that you can find there. He also supplies many restaurants and shops in town, and you will often see Cory at several of the community and culinary events that Victoria hosts. When I think of the little shops around town that are the epitome of a neighborhood go-to, The Whole Beast is high on my list.

A few of my favourite hand-crafted items found at the shop are Cory's *Salami Limone e Finocchiona* (lemon fennel salami) and the Duck Terrine with Porcini. Both are unbelievable. Right next door, in the same building, is the Village Butcher, a little shop that Cory also has a hand in. (Makes sense, right? Pig → butcher → charcuterie.) In addition to great meat, poultry, stocks and specialty items, you can also find local eggs, smoked cheese, and assorted fats. Namely, everything required to make The Whole Beast Hash (see page 281).

THE WHOLE BEAST

2032
OAK BAY AVENUE
→ thewholebeast.ca →
250.590.7675

The Whole Beast Hash

> This is Cory's version of skillet hash with baked eggs, using meat and smoked cheese from his shops, The Whole Beast and The Village Butcher. (It is not for the weak of heart, but it is so delicious). You can add a few more eggs to the basic recipe if the guests keep trickling in.

If using beef stock, pour it into a large pot and bring to a boil over medium-high heat. Turn down the heat to a simmer, and continue to cook, uncovered, over low heat for about 1 hour, stirring occasionally, or until reduced to about ½ cup.

Line a sheet pan with paper towel.

Fill a large pot with water and place it over high heat. Add the vinegar and salt and bring to a boil. Add the diced potatoes and cook for about 10 minutes. Drain the potatoes well and set aside on the prepared sheet pan to cool and dry out.

In a large, heavy ovenproof frying pan (cast iron is best), fry the bacon over medium-high heat for 5–7 minutes, until brown and almost crisp. Add the brisket and sausage and fry for another 5–7 minutes, until brown and the bacon is crisp. Remove the meat with a slotted spoon and set aside in a bowl, leaving all the fat in the pan.

Increase the temperature to medium-high to warm the fat and add the potatoes and rosemary. Season with salt and pepper to taste and fry until golden brown on all sides. You may need to add more fat to the pan if the potatoes soak it up too fast. Use whatever fat you have on hand—bacon fat, duck fat, lard and oil all work well. Remove the potatoes from the pan and set aside in a large bowl.

Bring the frying pan back up to medium-high heat and add the olive oil. Add the onion and sauté for 5–7 minutes, until light brown. Add the bell pepper, kale and mushrooms and sauté for about 10 minutes, until tender. Season to taste with more salt and pepper. Return the meat and potatoes to the pan along with the reduced beef stock (or demi-glace, or leftover gravy) and mix everything together well.

Preheat the oven to 400°F.

Make four small wells in the hash and crack a whole egg into each well. Sprinkle the cheese over everything and bake until the eggs are done to your liking—about 12 minutes for a soft yolk. Remove from the oven, top with scallions and fresh cracked pepper and serve with your favourite vinegary hot sauce.

4 cups beef stock (or ½ cup demi-glace or leftover gravy)
¼ cup white vinegar
2 Tbsp kosher salt
4 large Yukon Gold potatoes, skins on, cut into 1-inch dice (red-skinned potatoes work well too)
7 oz thick-sliced smoked side bacon, cut into 1-inch pieces
5½ oz thick-sliced smoked beef brisket, cut into 1-inch pieces
7 oz Andouille sausage, cut into ½-inch rounds
1 Tbsp fresh rosemary leaves, roughly chopped
Salt and ground black pepper
2 Tbsp extra virgin olive oil
½ medium red onion, cut into 1-inch dice
1 medium red bell pepper, cut into 1-inch dice
1 bunch of lacinato (black) kale, tough stems removed, cut width-wise into ¼-inch slices
3½ oz fresh shiitake mushrooms, cleaned and sliced in half
4 large eggs
¾ cup grated smoked cheddar
3 scallions, chopped
Your favourite vinegary hot sauce, to serve

THE
FOLKS
Who Know
BEST

Have you ever wondered why bacon is such a popular breakfast food? Or how to best put together a well-balanced cheese plate? Or how to get the most out of that wonderful tea you've just purchased? I know I have. So, I sat down with some of our town's experts on all the brunch basics and asked them for their best facts, tips, methods and processes.

The Bread Expert

BOND BOND'S BAKERY
bondbondsbakery.com

Rich Harrison

There is no question that bread in some form is a breakfast staple in kitchens all over the world. From the Chinese youtiao (a long deep-fried strip of dough) to Spanish churros, tortillas in Mexico and French croissants, flour, water and yeast are always a safe bet. Whether baked fried, grilled, boiled or steamed dough, either sweet or savoury, bread is something we're all familiar with.

Our bread expert, Rich Harrison, has spent his entire career working in kitchens, starting at age 14 as a dishwasher and working his way up to chef by the time he was 24. His passion for bread making began in 2006 when he and his wife, Jeneen, took over Bond Bond's Bakery in downtown Victoria.

Bakers need to learn how dough works in different conditions and how to adjust the ingredients in order to keep it consistent. Rich thanks his obsessive tendencies for his ability to continually achieve this, and seeing as Bond Bond's is a busy and buzzing business in a highly competitive town, it seems that we are thankful, too. "When it comes to bread making," Rich says, "the learning never ends."

When I asked Rich for recommendations on bread at brunch-time, he shared his favourites: for savoury bread, a cheese and onion scone; for sweet bread, a Danish-style cinnamon bun.

While whirly curls of dough with fruit baked in them and icing slathered on top, cheese-baked crusts and herbed, buttered flaky things are always a welcome addition to our table, let us not forget the good old standby, and one of the most common breakfast items in North America: toast. The word *toast* comes from the Latin word *tostum*, which means burnt or scorched. It is believed that burning was a means of preserving bread during the Roman Empire. While we have become much more sophisticated in terms of how we toast our bread (although on a rock by the fire is still perfectly acceptable), it remains simple and easy morning fare. Here are a few tips to enjoy bread at its best:

- **SHORT-TERM STORAGE:** Bread should be stored in a plastic bag or wrapping for 3–4 days at room temperature. Never store bread in the refrigerator. To reheat: For crusty bread, place unwrapped loaf directly onto oven rack and bake 4–8 minutes in a 350°F oven. For a soft crust, spray the top of the loaf lightly with water, enclose in foil and bake 6–10 minutes in a 300°F oven. Never reheat bread in a microwave!

- **FREEZING:** If you need to store fresh bread for more than 3–4 days, wrap it in a plastic bag as tightly as possible. Frozen breads without preservatives will remain good up to 3 weeks. When you're ready to use it, thaw and bring to room temperature or reheat.

- **REHEATING:** For crusty bread, place the unwrapped loaf directly onto the oven rack and bake for 4–8 minutes in a 350°F oven. For a soft crust, spray the top of the loaf lightly with water, wrap tightly in foil and bake for 6–10 minutes in a 300°F oven. Never reheat bread in a microwave!

The Cheese Expert

OTTAVIO
ottaviovictoria.com

Andrew Moyer

I could sit and talk cheese with Andrew Moyer of Ottavio Italian Bakery and Delicatessen for days. Not only is he well-rounded and insightful on the topic, it is clear he also enjoys sitting over an espresso and delving deeper into it all.

Andrew and his wife, Monica, opened Ottavio in 1997 in Oak Bay Village. They catered to cheese and charcuterie lovers, offering about 10 basic cheeses, bread, pastries, sandwiches and espresso. When customers inquired about different cheeses that they had tried elsewhere in the past, Andrew would write down their name and number in a notebook, source the cheese and eventually get it in to the shop. Imagine the customer's surprise when six months later they'd get a phone call saying their cheese was in! It was this sort of routine that made Andrew aware that the love of cheese was out there and at that time, the place to buy it in Victoria was not. He began to educate his customers, and slowly expanded our tastes to appreciate the more complex and intense cheeses from Italy, France, Quebec, Spain and more.

In 2003, Andrew and Monica took over an old, run-down hippy-style duplex, allowing them to expand their rotating cheese selection to around 220 different types (about 150 at any one time). Ottavio offers a great variety of products these days; however, cheese remains a specialty.

While adding cheese to any brunch recipe is encouraged, a wonderful way to enjoy cheese is by assembling a cheese plate. Choose three to five cheeses, bring them to room temperature before serving, and add some complementary flavours to the plate, such as fresh or dried fruit, compotes or marmalades, nuts, honey and fresh herbs. Be sure to keep the delicious rind on a soft cheese (trust me), though the rind on a hard cheese can be removed, as it is often a bit tough (think Parmesan).

Andrew recommends the following as a good start to a well-rounded cheese plate. If these particular cheeses are not available, talk to any of the cheese ambassadors at Ottavio and they can suggest a substitute.

- **FRESH CHEESE:** Often rindless, creamy and soft, it has a mild texture, but a full flavour profile. Recommended brand: Grey Owl from Quebec.
- **BLUE CHEESE:** Typically a richer, slightly salty cheese with a distinct flavour. Blues vary in texture, though a creamier blue will complement the selection of cheeses on this plate. Recommended product: Tiger Blue, a cow's milk cheese, from BC's Poplar Grove or St. Agur from France.
- **SURFACE RIPENED CHEESE:** Soft cheese, milky and tangy. Recommended product: Casatica di Bufala (buffalo milk cheese) from Italy—remember to eat the rind!
- **HARD CHEESE:** A more firm consistency with a stronger, nuttier flavour, such as sheep's milk cheese. Recommended product: Ossau Iraty from France.
- **WASHED RIND:** A soft to semi-firm cheese, this has rich flavour and is a little funky on the nose. Recommended product: Langres from France.

The Bacon Expert

THE WHOLE BEAST
thewholebeast.ca

Cory Pelan

Believe it or not, bacon became a breakfast staple thanks to a marketing campaign in the 1920s. A producer of everything pork (and many other popular food items), the Beech-Nut Packing Company desired an increase in consumer demand for bacon. Bernays was the advertising agency tasked with making this happen and approached their company doctor to ask if people might benefit from a heavier breakfast each day. The doctor "confirmed" (wink-wink) that they would and spread the word to his doctor friends, asking them in turn to encourage their patients to consume a breakfast of bacon and eggs to benefit their health. And so the somewhat sketchy popularity of bacon for breakfast was born.

It's hard to believe that that was almost 100 years ago, as we have seen bacon flit in and out of favour over the decades. In more recent years, we've seen bacon doughnuts, bacon in cocktails and even bacon ice cream, confirming its huge comeback. Not that you need to tell Cory Pelan any of this—he sells almost 200 pounds of his rosemary maple bacon per week.

Cory owns The Whole Beast Artisan Salumeria, where he produces an amazing line of authentic and original cured meat products and preserves. I met Cory several years ago when he was the chef at La Piola—a restaurant that is no longer, but one that definitely left its mark. Cory found that to get the best quality sausage, charcuterie, and other 'nose-to-tail'

products, he had to make them himself, and realized it was time to take this practice to the next level. That's when The Whole Beast was born. The accolades he's received since are certainly well deserved.

Now, back to that rosemary maple bacon I mentioned earlier. Cory dry-cures his bacon, creating a slice that cooks well and has less shrinkage than a more traditional wet-cured or brined bacon. He adds only a touch of maple, so as not to make it too sweet, and hints of a light hickory flavour can also be detected. The pork belly that eventually becomes the bacon comes from a local island farm.

To keep bacon as fresh as possible, it should be wrapped tightly in waxed paper, then plastic wrap and kept in the refrigerator for up to a week. Or freeze it for up to 3 months, wrapped the same way then sealed in a freezer bag.

Instead of making a big mess on the stove, Cory suggests you bake your bacon in the oven on a parchment-lined baking sheet, at 350°F, turning once or twice, for 15–20 minutes. This also allows you to focus on frying, poaching or scrambling your eggs while the bacon is cooking, rather than having to hover, as with the traditional pan-on-stove method. Be sure to drain cooked bacon on a paper towel–lined plate to catch the extra fat. Despite its shady beginnings, bacon has retained its salty, smoky popularity with most folks. However, if it's not your thing, talk to Cory about sausages or ham or other brunchy meat products. He is after all, an expert.

Jen and Ian Woike are the hard workers behind Farmer Ben's Eggs. A family-run business in the Cowichan Valley on Vancouver Island, Farmer Ben's has been supplying the area with eggs for over 40 years. Here, they share some facts and tips all about eggs, their production, and how to know if you've purchased the best.

For over 50 years in Canada, the use of steroids and hormones in egg-laying hens has been banned. Hens are typically vaccinated when they are young to build up their defences against disease, so medication is rarely used.

Eggs are six days old, on average, when they reach the grocery store. We track this in Canada through a regimented grading process. Eggs have 35 days of shelf life at the time of grading, and rather than being stored for weeks on end in warehouses, they move through an efficient process from farm to table, which ensures a fresh wholesome egg supply for all Canadians. All eggs sold in Canadian grocery stores are Grade A eggs. In order to be qualified as a Grade A egg, the shell must be clean, free of cracks and of a standard shape. The egg must have a firm white and the yolk must be centred inside the egg, confirmed during the grading process by being passed in front of a bright light making the insides of the egg visible. In other words, a Grade A egg is a fresh, quality egg that is as close to perfect as you can get!

A fresh egg will have a small air cell (less than 5 mm deep), which becomes larger as an egg ages. As time goes by, the firm round yolk becomes larger, flatter and more fragile. The thick white becomes thinner and more watery.

To test the freshness of your egg before cooking it, place it in a full bowl of cool water. A fresh egg will not float, but because the aforementioned air cell becomes larger as an egg ages, an older egg will. These eggs are still safe to eat, but it's best if they are hard-boiled or used in baking.

Eggs, like many other perishable foods, should be stored in the refrigerator to help maintain their freshness. The lower and consistent temperature of the refrigerator limits moisture loss through the pores of the egg shell.

There is no difference in nutritional value between an egg with a brown shell and one with a white shell. Flavour or cooking functionality is also not affected by the shell colour. The egg shell colour is determined by the breed of chicken. At Farmer Ben's, brown eggs are laid by the brown Rhode Island Red hens and white eggs are laid by the White Leghorns. The colour of the hen's ear area is the indicator, with a white or light spot meaning white eggs. The brown chickens are larger and require more food, which is why brown eggs may cost more than white eggs.

The Coffee Expert

CAFFE FANTASTICO

caffefantastico.com

Derek Allen

I hear coffee roaster Derek Allen throw around such words as approachable, uncomplicated, welcoming and easy-to-wake-up-to. Though she may be all of these things, in this case, he is not talking about his wife. He is talking about coffee, and the importance of these characteristics in a good harmonious cup.

Derek has been a roaster at Caffe Fantastico for 12 years, after having spent four years as a barista there. Suffice it to say that he is well versed in the topic of coffee, all the way from the tree to the cup. He has always been deeply interested in the pure flavours and unique qualities of the coffee bean, the regions it's grown in and the farmers who grow it. Derek has a great relationship with the producers who grow coffee for Fantastico, and the respect he has for them and the beans they grow comes through in the cup sitting in front of you. This is farm to table at its best.

Derek suggests a straightforward, easy-drinking, balanced coffee in general, though this is particularly relevant in a brunch scenario, as this will complement both sweet and savoury dishes and work for a wide range of tastes. A strong, dark, bitter cup of coffee is fine, of course, but pairing it with things like eggs and hollandaise would be akin to pairing a big leggy cabernet with a mild flaky fish.

A coffee bean is actually the seed inside the fruit from a tree, so like any stone fruit, it is at the mercy of conditions set forth by Mother Nature as well as the farmer who tends to it. This means that the processor's (that's Derek) skill and technique in drawing out the flavour characteristics is paramount for a good end result. Derek's ability to coax the natural flavours from the bean and not mask them is what makes his coffee great. He concerns himself with aroma, body, mouth-feel, after-taste, flavour and acidity, among other things.

Many steps go into making an exceptional cup of coffee. The last step is how we brew it. Derek suggests the following:

- Use coffee within 3 weeks of the roast date.
- Use fresh water that is filtered using a carbon filter. Water temperature should ideally be just off boiling, around 200°F. (Boil a kettle, then let the water rest for a minute or two before pouring it over the ground beans.)
- Grind just before brewing to capture the most aroma and flavour potential.
- Use a coffee to water ratio of about 2 level Tbsp of ground coffee per 6 oz of water.
- Grind size and brew time correlate: as grind size increases, so does brew time. For example:

EXPRESSO	very fine	20–30 sec.
AEROPRESS	fine medium	2–2½ min
DRIP COFFEE MACHINE (4–8 cup)	medium-coarse	4–6 min
FRENCH PRESS	medium-coarse	4–5 min

For more tips, visit caffefantastico.com/brewing-guide.

The Tea Expert

SILK ROAD TEA
silkroadteastore.com

Daniela Cubelic

Daniela is the beautiful and brilliant mastermind behind Silk Road Tea. Since 1992, she has been creating premium-quality organic teas that satisfy our souls and our taste buds alike. By using no additives such as sweeteners or artificial flavours or colours, it is clear that Daniela is interested in immersing us in a healthful and high-vibration line of teas. You can see the purity and rawness in many of Silk Road's loose leaf products. In their chai, for example, you can see whole cardamom pods and bits of cinnamon bark. Just smelling it warms the soul. The Angelwater tea contains rose petals, lavender, spearmint and elderflowers and certainly lives up to its secondary name of "tea of serenity." Once you've tried any of Daniela's teas, you'll find tea becomes a welcome part of your everyday life. Drinking tea, at least for me, is a ritual. It's a wake-up in the morning or a stop in the day, and not a day goes by when I don't drink at least one cup. Brewing tea properly is crucial to get the most from it.

How to brew your tea depends on what type you're making. Green, black, oolong and white tea all come from the same plant, but they are manufactured differently, which changes the chemical composition of the plant and also how it should be prepared. Herbal teas are caffeine-free blends of herbs.

- For **HERBAL TEA**, use water at a full rolling boil and steep for 7–10 minutes.
- For **BLACK TEA**, use water at a full rolling boil and steep for 2–5 minutes.
- For **OOLONG TEA**, use water just at the boil and steep for 5–7 minutes.
- For **WHITE TEA**, use water just before the boil and steep for 3–5 minutes.
- For **GREEN TEA**, use water just before the boil and steep for 1–3 minutes.

By following these brewing instructions, you are ensuring maximum health benefits and best flavour. When brewing green tea, if you use water that is too hot, you "overcook" the tea, which leads to a loss of nutrients and a bitter taste. When brewing black tea, the opposite is true. To get great flavour, use water at a full, rolling boil or you won't get good a flavour release from your black tea. Steeping tea for too long can lead to bitterness.

Tea Latte
MAKES 1 CUP

Tea lattes are the ultimate, cozy brunch drink. They are easy to make, but you should be aware of a couple of tips.

Never steep the tea directly in milk. Tea's flavour extracts well in water, but fats and other compounds in milk inhibit flavour release.

Use equal parts milk and brewed tea to make a tea latte. Milk will overwhelm the taste of tea if you use too much.

Brew 1 tsp tea in ½ cup water, using the recommended water temperature and steeping time for the type of tea you're making.

Heat ½ cup milk or non-dairy milk in a pot over low to medium heat—it can easily scorch. Continually whisk the milk while it is heating to create a foam.

When the tea has finished steeping, strain it into the pot. Whisk to combine, then pour into mugs. Add sweetener if desired.

Metric Conversions Chart

VOLUME

⅛ tsp	0.5 mL	3 cups	750 mL
¼ tsp	1 mL	3½ cups	875 mL
½ tsp	2.5 mL	4 cups/1 quart	1 L
¾ tsp	4 mL	4½ cups	1.125 L
1 tsp	5 mL	5 cups	1.25 L
1½ tsp	7.5 mL	5½ cups	1.375 L
2 tsp	10 mL	6 cups	1.5 L
1 Tbsp	15 mL	6½ cups	1.625 L
4 tsp	20 mL	7 cups	1.75 L
2 Tbsp	30 mL	8 cups	2 L
3 Tbsp	45 mL	12 cups	3 L
¼ cup/4 Tbsp	60 mL	¼ fl oz	7.5 mL
5 Tbsp	75 mL	½ fl oz	15 mL
⅓ cup	80 mL	¾ fl oz	22 mL
½ cup	125 mL	1 fl oz	30 mL
⅔ cup	160 mL	1½ fl oz	45 mL
¾ cup	185 mL	2 fl oz	60 mL
1 cup	250 mL	3 fl oz	90 mL
1¼ cups	310 mL	4 fl oz	125 mL
1½ cups	375 mL	5 fl oz	160 mL
1¾ cups	435 mL	6 fl oz	185 mL
2 cups/1 pint	500 mL	8 fl oz	250 mL
2¼ cups	560 mL	24 fl oz	750 mL
2½ cups	625 mL		

WEIGHT

1 oz	30 g
2 oz	60 g
3 oz	90 g
¼ lb/4 oz	125 g
5 oz	150 g
6 oz	175 g
½ lb/8 oz	250 g
9 oz	270 g
10 oz	300 g
¾ lb/12 oz	375 g
14 oz	400 g
1 lb	500 g
1½ lb	750 g
2 lb	1 kg
2½ lb	1.25 kg
3 lb	1.5 kg
4 lb	1.8 kg
5 lb	2.3 kg
5½ lb	2.5 kg
6 lb	2.7 kg

LENGTH

⅛ inch	3 mm
¼ inch	6 mm
⅜ inch	9 mm
½ inch	1.25 cm
¾ inch	2 cm
1 inch	2.5 cm
1½ inches	4 cm
2 inches	5 cm
3 inches	8 cm
4 inches	10 cm
4½ inches	11 cm
5 inches	12 cm
6 inches	15 cm
7 inches	18 cm
8 inches	20 cm
8½ inches	22 cm
9 inches	23 cm
10 inches	25 cm
11 inches	28 cm
12 inches	30 cm

CAN SIZES

4 oz	114 mL	19 oz	540 mL
14 oz	398 mL	28 oz	796 mL

OVEN TEMPERATURES

40°F	5°C	150°F	66°C	225°F	107°C	400°F	200°C
120°F	49°C	155°F	68°C	250°F	120°C	425°F	220°C
125°F	51°C	160°F	71°C	275°F	140°C	450°F	230°C
130°F	54°C	165°F	74°C	300°F	150°C	475°F	240°C
135°F	57°C	170°F	77°C	325°F	160°C	500°F	260°C
140°F	60°C	180°F	82°C	350°F	180°C		
145°F	63°C	200°F	95°C	375°F	190°C		

Acknowledgments

First and foremost, I want to thank Gary Hynes of *EAT* magazine. Back in 2007, he took a chance on a food-loving photographer and essentially introduced me to the expansive culinary scene here in Victoria and beyond. It is because of that exposure that I am where I am today.

Thank you to my friends and family, not only for their love, support and encouragement, but also for taking on such missions as "eating a different breakfast sandwich every day" because I most certainly couldn't trust only my own taste buds. They also deserve special kudos for obliging on all the occasions I have requested we get together, make copious amounts of food and photograph the whole ordeal. Oh, and for modelling for me countless times. And meeting me for brunch. You've done a lot. Endless thank-yous. An extra-special shout-out to the Brunch Potluck crew on page 194–195. To John and Dawn for opening your incredible home to us and being such culinary geniuses, and to Mel, Todd, Renate, Matt, and Jen for your exceptional cooking and cocktail-making skills.

Cassandra Anderton, Danielle Acken, Ally Parker, Jewleana Marens, Mands Burdette, Jill Van Gyn, Todd Wellman, Melanie Wagner-Collins and Dawn Thiessen for your recipe testing. Seriously—could not have gotten it done without you!

All the restaurant staff who struck a pose, gave me a smile, held up plates of food and props and reflectors and somehow contributed to the photos in this book with no warning at all that I was even coming their way.

Heidi Fink, for her enthusiasm in life and cooking and for the suggestion that got me started on this book-writing path.

My wonderful publisher, Taryn Boyd, for her faith in me and for allowing me such creative freedom. Also for being super cool and fun to hang out with. The entire stellar team at Touchwood Editions for all their hard work. It amazes me how many hands and hearts go into such a project.

Lesley Cameron, editor extraordinaire, whose experience and expertise was instrumental in the putting together of this book.

Tree Abraham for her beautiful design that helped bring this book to life.

Chintz and Co. for their gorgeous dishware featured at the brunch potluck, and Erika Arbour Nevins for her beautiful handmade Wicked Wanda pottery that is showcased multiple times in this book. It is my favourite collection.

And finally, the extensive number of Victoria restaurateurs, chefs and shop owners who put their trust in me to deliver a beautiful book, representative of our fine city. Thanks to you always.

Notes

Epigraph (page 3): This is a take on a quote from Ron Swanson of *Parks and Recreation* fame. Its origin is rather murky as it appears attributed to many sources and despite my best efforts I was unable to confirm its first appearance in the world.

Introduction (page 9): John Catucci, "Victoria Declared Brunch Capital of Canada by Food Network," March 12, 2016 (cbc.ca/news/canada/british-columbia/victoria-brunch-capital-1.3488472)

Bacon (page 289): The American Table, "How 'Bacon and Eggs' Became the American Breakfast," July 19, 2012 (americantable.org/2012/07/how-bacon-and-eggs-became-the-american-breakfast/) and Fanatic Cook, "When and Why Did Americans Start Eating Bacon and Eggs for Breakfast?," May 05, 2015 (fanaticcook.com/2015/05/05/when-and-why-did-americans-start-eating-bacon-and-eggs-for-breakfast)

Agrius's Carried Away (page 23) by Brooke Levie

Bourbon Mint Iced Tea (page 201) by Melanie Wagner-Collins

Dutch Baby with Fruit Compote (page 199) by Renate Wellman

Fuego's Michelada (page 73) by Shawn Soole

Grits with Beer-Braised Shrimp and Smoky Potatoes (page 211) by Melanie Wagner-Collins

Mount Royal Bagels with Spicy Smoked Salmon Spread (page 205) by Dawn Thiessen

Northern Quarter's Breakfast Uppercut (page 113) by Tim Siebert

Revive Brunch Smoothie (page 197) by Todd Wellman

Sakura Maru Cocktail (page 207) by Dawn Thiessen, adapted from NoMad NYC

Salsa Macha (page 245) by Pati Jinich, patijinich.com/recipe/salsa-macha

Sausage and Smoked Cheddar Strata (page 203) by Matt Polera

Spinach Quiche with Bacon (page 209) by Jennifer Letham-Sobkin

Vis à Vis Once Upon a Swizzle (page 171) by Jared Wegenast

Index

TouchWood Editions
103–1075 Pendergast Street
Victoria, BC V8V 0A1
TouchWoodEditions.com

The information in this book is true and complete to the best of the author's knowledge.
All recommendations are made without guarantee on the part of the author or the publisher.

Editing by Lesley Cameron
Cover and interior design by Tree Abraham

LIBRARY AND ARCHIVES CANADA CATALOGUING IN PUBLICATION
Wellman, Rebecca, author
First, we brunch / Rebecca Wellman.
Includes index.

Issued in print and electronic formats.
ISBN 978-1-77151-231-2 (softcover).—ISBN 978-1-77151-232-9
(HTML).—ISBN 978-1-77151-233-6 (PDF)
1. Cooking, Canadian—British Columbia style.
2. Cooking—British Columbia—Victoria. 3. Brunches.
4. Cookbooks. I. Title.
TX715.6.W45 2017   641.59711'28   C20179029665
                                                C20179029673

We acknowledge the financial support of the Government of Canada through the Canada
Book Fund and the province of British Columbia through the Book Publishing Tax Credit.

Canadä

This book was produced using FSC®-certified, acid-free papers, processed chlorine free,
and printed with soya-based inks.

Printed in Canada at Friesens

21 20 19 18 17   5 4 3 2 1